THIRD EDITION

HOW TO BUY
Foreclosed
Real Estate

For a Fraction of Its Value

THIRD EDITION

HOW TO BUY
Foreclosed
Real Estate

For a Fraction of Its Value

Theodore J. Dallow with Don Ayer and Dick Pas

BUSINESS

avon, massachusetts

Published by Adams Business, an imprint of
Adams Media, an F+W Publications Company
57 Littlefield Street, Avon, MA 02322. U.S.A.
www.adamsmedia.com

ISBN 10: 1-59869-669-6
ISBN 13: 978-1-59869-669-1

Printed in Canada.

J I H G F E D C B A

Library of Congress Cataloging-in-Publication Data
is available from the publisher.

This publication is designed to provide accurate and authoritative information with
regard to the subject matter covered. It is sold with the understanding that the publisher is not engaged in rendering legal, accounting, or other professional advice. If
legal advice or other expert assistance is required, the services of a competent professional person should be sought.
> —From a *Declaration of Principles* jointly adopted by a Committee of the
> American Bar Association and a Committee of Publishers and Associations

Many of the designations used by manufacturers and sellers to distinguish their product are claimed as trademarks. Where those designations appear in this book and
Adams Media was aware of a trademark claim, the designations have been printed
with initial capital letters.

This book is available at quantity discounts for bulk purchases.
For information, please call 1-800-289-0963.

Contents

xi   **FOREWORD**

1   **PART ONE**
     How Did We Get Here?

3   **CHAPTER 1**
     If 75 Million People Lose, Say, $35,000 Each, Is That a
     Good Day at the Office?

5   **CHAPTER 2**
     Moving on to Mortgage Lending

10   **CHAPTER 3**
     Important Recent History

20   **CHAPTER 4**
     The Rise and Fall of Subprime Lending

26   **CHAPTER 5**
     How Foreclosures Happen

33   **CHAPTER 6**
     Payment Option Loans and Other Loan Types

37   **CHAPTER 7**
     The Best Mortgage Loan and the Second-Best Mortgage
     Loan

40   **CHAPTER 8**
     Other Reasons for Foreclosure

47   **CHAPTER 9**
     Deed in Lieu of Foreclosure

53   **PART TWO**
      How to Buy Foreclosed and Distressed Properties

55   **CHAPTER 10**
      You Have to Know the Numbers

60   **CHAPTER 11**
      Preforeclosure—Contacting Mortgagors Prior to the Sale

67   **CHAPTER 12**
      Acquire Knowledge and Avoid Emotional Pitfalls

70   **CHAPTER 13**
      Short Sales

74   **CHAPTER 14**
      Before the Sale

86   **CHAPTER 15**
      Preparing for the Sale

91   **CHAPTER 16**
      The Sale

98   **CHAPTER 17**
      After the Sale

106   **CHAPTER 18**
      Calculating a Bid Price for Investment Property

110   **CHAPTER 19**
      Investment Real Estate

117   **CHAPTER 20**
      Managing Investment Real Estate

122   **CHAPTER 21**
      Those Easy-Money, No-Cash Commercials and Seminars

129   **PART THREE**
The Road Ahead

131   **CHAPTER 22**
Fear and Greed

136   **CHAPTER 23**
Fine-Tuning Your Thinking

139   **CHAPTER 24**
We Didn't Know Mortgages and Real Estate Were
That Important

143   **APPENDIX A**
Frequently Asked Questions

151   **APPENDIX B**
Checklists

159   **APPENDIX C**
Standard Buyer's Agreement

165   **APPENDIX D**
Glossary of Crucial Terms

173   **INDEX**

176   **ABOUT THE AUTHORS**

Acknowledgments

The authors gratefully acknowledge
the skill and enthusiasm of B. K. Nelson.

Foreword

REAL ESTATE SOARED and real estate plunged. The summer of 2007 saw the nation's highest rate of foreclosures in the forty-four years recorded by the national Mortgage Bankers Association. According to the association, 5.06 percent of mortgage customers in the United States are delinquent and 1.4 percent are in foreclosure.

As one newspaper headline read, "We're not out of the woods yet." Headlines similar to this are appearing all over the nation. They were a long time coming. The recent historic real estate boom originated in a very long period of low interest rates (by recent standards). The Federal Reserve began an historic drop of short-term interest rates in mid-May 2000. They continued to reduce these rates (sharply after the September 11, 2001, terrorist attacks) until interest rates reached their low point in late June 2003. On July 1, 2004, the Federal Reserve began the first of seventeen quarter-percent interest rate increases, continuing through late June 2006. Rates held at that level until the September 18, 2007, half a percentage point reduction. The Great Real Estate Boom was a lagging but highly powerful response to low interest rates. The Great Boom began at various dates in various markets but was raging in most real estate markets by 2003. The Great Fall likewise became apparent at different dates in different markets but was widespread by mid-2005, later in some markets. The boom was fueled by widespread availability of subprime and nonconventional loans and a general consensus that real estate values would continue to soar. Home ownership in the United

States reached a historic high in 2004 when 69 percent of the population owned their own homes.

The end of the real estate boom actually had its origins with that first of seventeen consecutive actions over the next two years by the Federal Reserve Open Market Committee. Those rising interest rates finally induced first a slowing housing market, then the Great Fall, aided and again accompanied by a mass psychological swing, this time *against* real estate acquisition and investment.

The lightning-fast collapse in early 2007 of much subprime lending was reinforced by a negative real estate market in most of the country. Some local real estate markets have held up quite well, with relative price stability and even price increases. Places in the Northwest like Portland and Seattle, some of the Carolinas, and the oil-boom town of Casper, Wyoming, come to mind. In other places, such as San Diego and much of the rest of California; Las Vegas, Nevada; much of Florida; Arizona; and large portions of Michigan, Ohio, and Indiana, real estate values have dramatically gone the other way.

With academics, trade-association economists, and government number-crunchers tossing off figures left and right, no one can be absolutely certain how many single-family properties in the United States will see foreclosure. Most experts do agree that the rate of financially distressed properties or foreclosures is unlikely to decline any time soon.

The ripples of the real estate crisis continue to spread. On September 11, 2007, the *Wall Street Journal* reported that Bear Stearns, a large Wall Street firm much in the headlines because of its large subprime lending involvement, had seen its share price drop 34 percent since the start of the year. Over the next two weeks, the Federal Reserve cut both discount and Fed funds rates by half a percent, and by September 23, Bear Stearns's share price had edged back to roughly a 28 percent drop undoubtedly aided by the September 18, 2007, half a percentage point interest rate cut.

These events have struck especially hard at the mortgage industry. In August 2007, several large mortgage firms that together had been responsible for the annual purchase of $118 billion in mortgage loans ceased operations. During a single week of that same month, six mortgage or financial firms cut 13,000 jobs, virtually all of them mortgage related.

Countrywide Financial Corporation, the nation's largest mortgage lender (or second-largest, depending on when or how the ranking was calculated) was once also a large subprime loan producer. In the late summer of 2007, Countrywide announced that for the time being, it was reducing its production of subprime mortgage loans. From that point onward, the only subprime loans it would produce were those mortgage loans that could be sold to either the Federal National Mortgage Association (Fannie Mae) or the Federal Home Loan Mortgage Corporation (Freddie Mac) or that could be insured by the Government National Mortgage Association (Ginnie Mae).

Countrywide's action came at a time when the entire secondary market for subprime and Alt-A mortgage loans (both discussed at length in Part One of this book) was in an unprecedented contraction, with hundreds of mortgage firms going under.

Wells Fargo Home Mortgage, another huge mortgage lender, made another important announcement in August 2007, saying its decisions on how the way it looked at pricing or even the availability of Alt-A mortgage loans would be made on a day-to-day basis. And the best source of information about mortgage-broker lending and mortgage-broker companies has said that by the end of 2008 the number of U.S. mortgage-broker firms is expected to decline by roughly one third. Over the past decade, mortgage-broker firms have made approximately 55 to 66 percent of the nation's mortgage loans.

Whatever views people may currently have about trends in residential real estate prices, it's clear that public perception of residential real estate prices in most of the United States has undergone a dramatic shift from "Of course they're going up" to "Whatever prices are doing, they sure aren't going up"—all of this in less than three years.

Buying foreclosures is an art. It is not the perfect job for everyone, but it is for some, and it might be for you. It is not easy, but the same can be said about almost anything else that's worth doing. Plus, for those who work to understand and master them, all tasks become easy after a while.

Many people will lose real estate to foreclosure. Many will acquire foreclosed real estate. This book will make you a stronger buyer of real estate, all real estate, and it will make you a more successful seller of real estate. It will also give you the background information you need to feel comfortable during those times when it's best to simply stand pat.

Who should read this book? Anyone who wants to make a profit or continue making a profit through the process of buying foreclosed real estate.

This book is the creation of three authors. In 1995, the late Ted Dallow wrote the highly successful first edition, which he revised and rewrote for a second edition published in 2000.

Don Ayer, a career real estate broker in Wisconsin, and Dick Pas, a mortgage banker and attorney, edited and updated this revised edition. In creating this third edition, the current authors have organized the book for three different types of readers. First, many readers have a serious interest in the genesis of the real estate boom and the subsequent collapse of the subprime lending market. These readers will learn more in this book about the powerful effect of the Federal Reserve and its policies on the supply of foreclosed and distressed properties, now and in the future.

The second group includes those readers who may have a limited interest in the forces controlling the real estate market; they are primarily interested in the best way to buy foreclosed and distressed real estate. Finally, the third group is comprised of the numerous readers with a desire to learn as much as they can about both of these subjects and to figure out what they need to do to make good economic decisions.

This "go to" book provides information on these crucial topics:

- It identifies the influential market factors that a foreclosed-property buyer must know; these are the same things the pros already know and use to make a profit buying foreclosed properties.
- It provides an overview of the real estate market in the United States and explains how real estate market conditions evolved into their current state. It describes the conditions to watch for in order to make good real estate decisions today. This book also describes what to watch for so you'll know where the real estate market will be next quarter, next year, and five years out.
- It explains the fundamental role that the Federal Reserve plays in the real estate market and how it contributes to good times and to bad times. Included in this discussion is an explanation of how lending functions.
- It outlines foreclosure procedures, which vary among states and locales within states, describes how buyers of foreclosed properties can quickly come up to speed in the jurisdictions that interest them, and explains the process known as *short sales*. This book also covers the topic of sales options and the best way to make good purchase decisions.
- It provides comprehensive, inexpensive information about the start-to-finish process of buying foreclosures. On any weekend day, in any city, the local papers feature big advertisements for seminars on how to buy foreclosures. This book is an inexpensive, effective alternative. It explains the structure and purpose of such seminars and how to deal with them.
- It provides a clear, easy-to-understand explanation of tax sales, information that most readers will be surprised to find is not only useful to the prospective buyer of foreclosed properties but interesting to boot.

- It provides plenty of information about a wide range of real estate topics—from inspections to foreclosure options to the inside scoop on those late-night television ads that promise to show the quick way to riches through real estate, even for people who don't have two quarters to rub together.
- It describes a smart way to make money in real estate for readers who may not have a lot of money to start. This book also provides readers with the means to protect their investments with the goal of helping them avoid losing tons of money.

This short book has all this information and much more. It gives you the science and art of making money buying foreclosed real estate. It takes you on an inside tour of the mortgage lending industry. You'll be treated to a VIP ride in the Fed limo, getting the information you need to know whether to tighten your seatbelt or sip champagne. After reading, you'll feel better about greed. And even fear. Promise.

As you read, you will see why all this information is here and why it's necessary for the foreclosed-property buyer to understand. You'll see that all of it in combination gives you an understanding of the big real estate picture, the full background to help you make the right decisions.

Our best regards to you. And pass them on.

T.D.

D.A.

D.P.

DISCLAIMER

This book is not legal advice.

It is recommended that you seek legal counsel in all of your real estate dealings. We certainly do. In our writings, we touch upon subjects that can and do vary in different parts of the United States. Because of the differences in foreclosure practices and procedures from state to state and even among various localities within a particular state, this book is not legal advice. Before taking action in any real estate matter, check with your attorney.

PART ONE

How Did We Get Here?

CHAPTER 1

If 75 Million People Lose, Say, $35,000 Each, Is That a Good Day at the Office?

THE FEDERAL GOVERNMENT estimates that there are 75 million single-family homes in the United States. For these homeowners, their home and other real estate holdings (typically a second home, a recreational property, or a small number of rental properties) constitute a significant portion of their net worth.

Equity in real estate is calculated according to the following formula: current market value, minus expenses of sale, minus debt against it (either purchase-money mortgages taken out to buy the property, or refinance loans or home equity loans). That equity can increase, stay flat, or decline. Remember those 75 million single-family homes? What happens to their value has huge implications, not only for the families that live in them but for the nation's economy.

For example, if a good portion of those 75 million properties now have, say, an average market value of $35,000 less than in mid-2005, the height of the last boom (a working estimate of the decline in the value of American single-family homes since the beginning of the decline in the real estate market), any calculator needs many digits to compute the total impact.

Sad to say, many homeowners might be relieved to learn that their homes had suffered a decline in market value of "only"

$35,000. Many homeowners have seen the value of their real estate tumble to far lower depths than this.

Common sense would suggest that along with such widespread drops in real estate values, U.S. consumers were curtailing their retail spending by a proportionate amount. Surprisingly, through mid-2007, the huge decline in real estate equity in many markets has failed to seriously curtail consumer spending, which has been remarkably strong in the face of these numbers. MasterCard, whose revenues are a significant measure of consumer spending, reported in mid-2007 that its first-quarter profits had soared by 70 percent, led by an almost 20 percent jump in the number of credit card and debit card transactions.

What has been going on? Do employment rates outweigh the impact of home values when the consumer decides whether or not to spend? Apparently so. It seems that consumers are adjusting to their changed circumstances, or at least had done so through mid-2007. Here's why consumer spending initially remained so robust. The fact is that it's hard to break previous spending patterns and habits, even if we want to. The majority of Americans spend a lot of time traveling in their cars, along American roadways lined on both sides with business establishments whose goal is to make them stop their cars, get out, and spend money without regard to their discretionary budgets.

Is it possible to make a discretionary real estate purchase when the conventional wisdom is that the local real estate market is flat or declining? Yes, but the large majority of people will not.

As economic beings, we are predominately creatures of habit, strongly influenced by conventional wisdom. If we understand that conventional wisdom can be self-fulfilling, we have very valuable information. By absorbing this and being aware of our own and others' habits, we can help make our own best economic decisions.

CHAPTER 2

Moving on to Mortgage Lending

OLD WESTERN MOVIES and some holiday movie classics may leave the impression that foreclosure actions arise from greed, heartlessness, and even pure malevolence. These movies make colorful tales, but there can be plenty of other reasons that properties go into foreclosure.

These days, mortgages have become big business. In this nation's retailing of everything from groceries to consumer electronics, appliances, home-improvement items, and gas for the car, the large firms now dominate. The same is true in the mortgage loan business. If you're in the market for a mortgage loan, you will find that the large mortgage loan servicers dominate.

Usually the source of a consumer's mortgage loan is a lender with a local office (such as a bank, savings bank, mortgage broker, mortgage banker, or credit union). The most aggressive lenders—that is, those most willing to lend—are mortgage brokers, who in recent years have made roughly two-thirds of all residential mortgage loans. Clearly, mortgage brokers have been leading the way in making loans to borrowers who were previously unqualified to acquire a home.

The vast majority of all these loans made by all lenders are now sold in the secondary market. And many of these mortgage loans are funded and purchased right "at the table" as the loan closes. This enables the local lender to have plenty of funds for the next borrower. Loans funded "at the table" use money from the next lender up the line so the local lender actually uses not even a dime of its own money.

Once mortgage loans have been made and sold, they are likewise "serviced." That is, they are administered in all aspects, including collecting payments, paying taxes and insurance (for loans with escrow accounts created to hold the funds to pay those items), collecting late fees, and dealing with delinquent borrowers—up to and including referring for foreclosure and even administering foreclosure. These mortgage loan administration activities are done by or on behalf of institutional investors who are almost always in a town or city other than the one where the real estate is located.

Even loans made by the local office of a multi-office bank chain and serviced by that bank chain have in all probability been sold and are being serviced for the institutional loan owner according to its directives, procedures, and requirements, including delinquency, default, and foreclosure aspects. And in many cases, the foreclosure processing, legal work, and property sale are handled by specialist firms serving a number of institutional investors (though the institutional loan servicer or loan owner retains some or all of policy- or final decision-making control).

The widespread institutionalization of mortgage lending in recent decades was launched by Congress with its creation of the following government-sponsored entities (GSEs): the Federal National Mortgage Association (FNMA), the Federal Home Loan Mortgage Corporation (FHLMC), and the Government National Mortgage Association (GNMA). These entities are known respectively as Fannie Mae, Freddie Mac, and Ginnie Mae. These GSEs were created to guarantee and purchase mortgage loans from local lenders so there would be sufficient funds for local lenders to continue lending in furtherance of the national goal of encouraging home ownership in the United States. Fannie Mae, Freddie Mac, and, to a lesser extent, Ginnie Mae have become household words because of the huge number of mortgages these entities purchase.

The GSEs play a huge role in providing liquidity (that is, plenty of funds) for mortgage lenders and borrowers. With their loan purchase requirements (or underwriting standards) and their automated loan-underwriting systems, the GSEs also play a huge role in establishing the borrower characteristics needed for approval of the loans they are purchasing. In the years before subprime or nonconforming loans were made on such a wide scale, a nonapproval by the underwriting system used by these entities meant the end of the road for a loan applicant at many local lenders. Some lenders still operate in that manner. However, the majority of lenders will now agree to lend if the GSE approval (agreement to guarantee/purchase a particular loan) is at a lower price to the lender (meaning the lender will charge the borrower a higher interest rate), or if another wholesale lender (such as a wholesale lender specializing in subprime loans) agrees to purchase that particular loan from the local lender. Local lenders very often require a favorable decision to purchase a particular loan before they will agree to "close that loan."

The Good Old Days?

Prior to the creation of the GSEs, before the widespread availability of funds for mortgage lending, and predating Congress's earlier creation of the Veterans Administration (VA) and Federal Housing Administration (FHA) low- or no-down-payment mortgage-loan guarantee programs, local lenders previously often had little or absolutely no money for mortgage lending. The Good Old Days of mortgage lending were hardly good in the eyes of most observers.

In the last decades of the nineteenth century and the first decades of the twentieth century, most buyers found that their home acquisition options were limited. They could chop logs or dig sod to build a house. They could pay cash for a house. Or they could hope they knew a banker who would agree to lend perhaps 50 percent of a home's purchase price if the banker liked them and was willing to lend them some of the bank's limited (often very limited) funds for a mortgage loan.

When all was said and done, about the only group that could be assured of mortgage loans was the group that played cards with the banker or the group whose spouses played cards with the banker's spouse. Mortgage lending was almost that tight.

The government determined that more widespread home ownership was in the public policy and financial interests of the United States, and it created low- or no-down-payment mortgage-loan guarantee programs for the FHA and the VA. The FHA program was initiated in the 1930s. The VA loan program was authorized for World War II vets in 1946. At this time, the government also created the Freddie Mac, Fannie Mae, and Ginnie Mae entities. The purpose of these GSEs was to guarantee other (non-FHA and non-VA) mortgage loans and to purchase those loans from local lenders to further assure that mortgage funds were readily available throughout the country. The GSEs also gathered the mortgages they purchased from local lenders into bundles or pools, which institutional investors then bought as passive investments.

These investments were passive because other entities serviced the mortgage loans (collecting payments and so on), an arrangement that continues to this day. The GSEs are not technically government agencies, but their guarantees are treated in the marketplace as if they were.

This all means that any particular mortgage loan is most likely part of a pool or bundle of mortgage loans. It is owned as part of that group of loans—that "bundle or pool"—by a large financial institution or investor. That institution or investor could be a bank, life insurance company, pension fund, college endowment, or even one of the new investment funds or so called hedge funds.

Wall Street firms first acted as sales agents for the GSEs, another role they still perform. These Wall Street firms then became highly creative in the use of the mortgage loans. Increasingly, these bundles or pools of mortgage loans backed up or became the collateral (the asset) behind new "mortgage backed securities." These new "mortgage-backed securities" became additional highly sophisticated offerings that appealed to institutional investors.

From the late 1990s through 2005, some of these investment options—dazzling in their complexity—fueled the rapidly expanding growth of subprime and nonconforming loan products available to lenders and borrowers at the local level. This also contributed to the run-up in real estate prices at that time.

Mortgage funds thus became increasingly available to an ever-expanding range of potential owner occupants and real estate investors. These mortgages were supplied by a mix of traditional and highly aggressive local lenders.

Even after the highly publicized subprime lender failures of early 2007 and the sharp subprime (nonconventional) loan contraction that followed, there were still more borrower opportunities for mortgage financing than was the case in all but a few years of the last century. Remember those card-playing days.

The principal characteristic of all recent mortgage lending is the involvement of large institutional investors at all stages of the loan process.

The point of all this background review is to help you understand that foreclosure and foreclosure option decisions are, in the huge majority of cases, made either by specialist firms or by specialist personnel of mortgage servicers working for or on behalf of large institutional investors.

It's all business (still with significant, maybe more, opportunities), and you'll need to be businesslike in any lender negotiation or sale after foreclosure in which you wish to be successful.

CHAPTER 3

Important Recent History

HOW DID WE GO from the Great Real Estate Boom that characterized the first half-decade of the twenty-first century to the Great Real Estate Bust that seems to have claimed the second half of the decade?

Let's take a look. Understanding what happened in recent years is essential to our being able to know which way real estate values will run at any time in the future.

How far back did the run up to the Great Real Estate Fall reach? The answer to that question depends somewhat on how you count, and also which real estate market your are watching

In recent decades, the United States has weathered more than a handful of crises that could have tanked the economy and the real estate market with it, including these:

- The collapse of the savings-and-loan industry of the 1980s
- The Asian financial crisis of the late 1990s
- The failure of Long-Term Capital Management in 1998—a failure so big and such a threatening loss that the Fed had to step in
- The terrorist attacks of September 11, 2001
- The dot-com boom and bust of 2000 and 2001, respectively

And, of course, there's the current crisis with subprime mortgages and what they are doing to other investments. In each case, the Federal Reserve dealt with the problem either by lowering interest rates, by adding reserves to the banking system, or by doing both. Always the Fed spoke reassuring words and made sure our banking system had enough liquidity with interest rates low enough to keep our economy from going into severe recession.

Had the Federal Reserve not acted as it did in these crises, we'd remember those events for having caused more economic pain than they generated in actuality.

After September 11, 2001, and the dot-com bust that followed soon after, the Fed took rates to the lowest level in a generation. It held rates low long enough to prevent any chance of an economic collapse and to foster the economic growth and recovery that followed.

The result of Federal Reserve actions was a remarkable economic record. Each of these crises could have produced a long lasting downturn. In the period of January of 2002 through mid-2007 our economy revived and grew. At the same time, inflation was firmly in check. What a remarkable record of accomplishment for the Fed—an accomplishment requiring cooperation of other central banks and financial institutions.

Pretty dazzling. So, how is it possible to back off from historic low rates while keeping inflation from running away and still keeping interest-rate-driven real estate markets from collapsing?

It Isn't Easy

The Fed gave it a go with seventeen consecutive quarter-percent raises at regularly scheduled Open Market Committee meetings. It also tried words and nudges and winks to those who would listen. Not everyone did. Most of us were too busy enjoying the Great Real Estate Boom.

We were lending, selling, buying, building, developing, speculating, appraising, surveying, supplying, and delivering. Did we overbuild? Did we bring too many subdivisions on line? Did we borrow too much? Did we lend too eagerly, with reduced down payments and lower asset and income criteria? We sure did.

There's no question that the real estate industry and regulators could have done more. Similarly, Wall Street could been more selective in its packaging and marketing of mortgage-backed investment securities. And hedge funds and other institutional investors should have been more selective in what they bought.

Caught up in the boom, municipalities issued too many subdivision approvals and building permits. Increasing numbers of people bought properties on speculation. Banks contributed by lending freely to builders and developers. And advisors and accountants held their tongues and did not give their best advice. The consequences of all this lack of fiscal caution have now come around to the housing market.

The Federal Reserve and Its Effect on You

Over the past decades, real estate industry and lending veterans and the broader public have seen many periodic cycles in both real estate market activity and price trends.

In most of these cycles, the predominant force turning the real estate weather vane has been short- and long-term interest rates and their direction. The Federal Reserve Open Market Committee directly controls two short-term rates. These short-term rates are the accelerator and the brake for real estate.

Indirectly, these short-term rates steer bond and long-term mortgage rates, sometimes quickly and sometimes with the slow pace of a large ship at sea. Surprisingly, a very powerful element of mass-market psychology sets in as well and often both accompanies and strongly reinforces cyclical swings in real estate market activity and how prices trend. It wasn't something in the air or water that caused the widespread euphoria and rampant speculation in residential real estate in 2003 and 2004. We were simply thinking alike and acting alike.

The force of this psychology never fails to impress us with both its strength and also its capacity to drive the real estate market out of proportion to the actual level of interest rates or other underlying economic causes. This herd wisdom nonetheless takes its lead from the direction of short-term rate movements by the Fed.

It could be argued that residential real estate is a local commodity driven by local economics and location. True enough. But if interest-rate swings are big enough, all but the very strongest and weakest metropolitan markets and individual properties move in the same general direction, as influenced by the level and direction of movement of short-term rates by the Federal Reserve.

The amount and percentage of capital moving into the U.S. real estate sector in the last years of the 1990s and the first half decade of this century almost certainly raised Federal Reserve worries about the relative shortage of investment capital available for industrial and other economy sectors.

New residential construction begun in that period likely constituted, in the Fed's view, an overallocation of both physical resources and capital to ultimately nonproducing or non–income-generating assets (single family housing), thus depriving other economic sectors that are capable of contributing more to the long-run strength of our economy.

Several additional arguments can be made with regard to Federal Reserve policy:

Federal Reserve Open Market Committee power and decisions can cause huge real estate market swings and even economic disruptions of such magnitude these decisions should not be made without public policy debate and input. In past decades, Federal Reserve policy decisions have been viewed as inscrutable, even mystical, and certainly beyond the general scope of debate, discussion, or even the feeblest of requests, recommendations, or demands from either the public or this country's elected leadership.

The Federal Reserve has been accorded this seemingly untouchable status because of many recent years of relatively stable prices without recession, a masterful performance acknowledged by even the harshest of the Fed's few critics.

These Federal Reserve policy decisions accelerate or brake real estate activity and investment to an extent that would be unacceptable if other asset sectors (stock market or employment levels for example) were similarly affected.

This brief section is provided so you realize the really big guy in any barroom brawl involving future trends in real estate is the Federal Reserve, our central bank, and its Open Market Committee. The future trends in question include the level of interest rates and their direction, the direction of lending policies for non-conventional (subprime) loans, and even the direction of lender policies with regard to distressed borrowers and their properties, which previously ended up in foreclosure.

A big component of the Fed's strength is its ability to influence Congress, the federal executive agencies, and even the president in the policies they enact into law and implement with respect to economic policy matters.

All this being said, there are now and will be for the foreseeable future lots of opportunities in real estate in your area.

Opportunities to acquire distressed real estate will swell. In fact, the simple fact of reading this book will mean better opportunities for you. Increased opportunities will also result once lenders, attorneys, loan administration personnel, judgment creditors, and others also begin to appreciate and accept the value of foreclosure alternatives for the wave of distressed property coming at us.

For municipal officials looking at future subdivision applications, modification requests, or zoning change demands, there will be an understanding that there are many options. For example, a developer may be able to negotiate with its lender. And a municipality may be better served by standing firm for its subdivision requirement than making a decision it will later regret. Some of these possible courses of action, maybe not even yet thought of, may provide much better opportunities for developers, lenders, and municipalities.

State officials will be sure to hear requests from builder's groups for waiver of environmental and other regulations. If state officials have a full knowledge of what is happening in real estate markets and lending, they will presumably be able to make better decisions.

Legislatures and Congress also will hear requests and demands from developers, builders, lenders, and consumer groups for waivers, regulation modifications, and relief from other requirements or taxes. Knowing the full background behind the demands could mean a much better legislative response.

Federal Reserve officials with a fuller understanding of the aftermath of use of their accelerator and brake (and their regulatory and persuasive powers) will be better positioned to steer the best course.

Neighbors, community organizations, and city officials likewise can make better decisions for their neighborhoods and cities knowing that for each property, there may be several options in addition to a foreclosure that is drawn out to its bitter end.

Human Cost of Foreclosure

In trying to find alternatives to foreclosure, municipal officials and lenders should consider not only the economic implications of foreclosure but also its human cost. The personal cost of foreclosure is enormous, not just in dollars but in its future effect on the individuals and families. Here is just one of thousands of examples.

In 1842, Don Ayer's great-grandfather and great-grandmother, as well as two other related couples, immigrated to Wisconsin from Durham County, England. They were not farmers in England, but they all landed on farms in Wisconsin.

Great-grandfather Ayer bought an eighty-acre parcel, he being the fourth owner of that farm. The original owner was a veteran named Goodfellow, who got it on a land grant signed by President Polk. Great-grandfather Ayer had five children, three boys and two girls. He not only developed the original homestead, but also bought two adjacent eighty-acre parcels, developed each with buildings, and staked three of the five kids in farming. One girl married a Catholic and was banished from the family. The oldest boy, John, wanted to join the army. Great-grandfather Ayer objected, so John left for South Dakota and developed three farms there.

Don Ayer's grandfather had three boys on his farm, and his son (Ayer's father) had six boys on that same farm. That farm was where the family lived from 1880 to 1945. In the early 1930s, that farm desperately needed a new barn, so Grandfather Ayer took out a mortgage at the local bank for $10,000, had a barn raising, and with the help of everyone around built a beautiful new barn and painted it barn red.

When the 1930s stock market crash and the Great Depression occurred, the family couldn't pay the bank, which started foreclosure proceedings. In 1937, a deed in lieu of foreclosure was recorded in the county seat, part of the stipulation being that the bank would never pursue any further legal action against Grandfather Ayer.

Don observes, "My father would never own real estate after that. He preached and preached to us six boys that if you borrow from a bank, they own it, not you, and they can and will take it back. In short he was a bitter man.

"That sermon set into my two oldest brothers. However, finally my oldest brother bought a house, finally. My point is that the effect of foreclosure is far reaching. Some families never recover, some take a generation to recover. The effect is long and far. This farm was not foreclosed, but the threat of foreclosure was strong enough to get Grandpa Ayer to sign a quit claim deed to end the threat and hassle. And this story is only one of millions." If you and those you share this book with have a sense that even one foreclosure on a block can have a strong negative effect on neighbors, that block, and even the neighborhood, you are right. Multiple foreclosures in a neighborhood can have devastating effects there and in the larger community.

And the pain of the parents, daughters and sons in the family that loses a single foreclosed home is real. The loss to municipalities, cities, states, lenders and investors, builders, developers, and all who own real estate in this country is huge. Like the costs of a long war, the true impact of the financially distressed properties in our land is still to come.

Let's step back and take a look at this crash from another perspective.

A Disastrous Elevator Ride

Imagine a big elevator.

The rise and fall of real estate in the first decade of the new millennium was unique in that it was not a secondary result of a general economic slowdown. Real estate led rather than followed the general economy. In recent decades, general business cycles carried real estate up or down the elevator, smoothly or with lurches. This rise and fall began with the brakes on the elevator starting to slip long before even most serious economic observers noticed. And the role of conventional wisdom was powerful indeed.

In the past, real estate passengers usually rode the elevator in a crowd behind or with most other passengers in the same up or down direction. This time, in the early twenty-first century, real estate passengers led. And a lot of those real estate passengers had just stopped at the refinance ATM on the third floor to get cash to spend along the way.

As the elevator went up, more passengers got on at each floor as the elevator stopped at hardware, appliance, power tools, even small construction equipment.

From the nearby office building came builders and developers, lenders, surveyors, and lots of real estate brokers. Attorneys and accountants came, along with appraisers and construction workers, as well as furniture movers from the building in the final construction phase next door.

Someone spotted a lumberyard owner, a tile maker, and truck drivers and gas station owners. There were huge numbers of property owners getting on the elevator now.

A growing number of speculators climbed aboard, and the cables began to creak. Behind them, in a hurry to catch up, was a big bunch of folks scurrying to make sure they didn't miss the car on the way up.

The treasurer of the town, who seemed to be smiling, came through the door.

Many in the crowd were busy, deep in cell phone conversations. Outside, the streets were filled with a blur of rushing traffic, and all seemed busy and happy.

It was taking quite a while for the elevator to get to the top floor. The car seemed to be slowing down. It was confusing. Some folks scurried around in the crowded space, talking to each other and on their cell phones.

Others started to wonder what they were doing. Why wasn't the car still going up, and why was it getting so quiet?

The car stopped at another floor, but no one got off. Instead, there was a crush at the open elevator doors as more people crowded in. The elevator was jammed with real estate people. The doors closed. And then, instead of going up, the elevator began to go down.

The car picked up speed as it whizzed past the floor with the walkway to the construction site; it accelerated even more past the floor connecting to the office building; and with a roar it flew past the hardware, appliances, lighting, and tools. The ATM was but a blur in the mad plunge.

The crowd outside heard the roar and screams as the elevator crashed into the sub-basement. The sad familiar scene of firemen, rescue squad, and police unfolded, and the newspapers first reported the wreckage and then sent in their investigative reporters to write the analysis stories.

The president and the biggest banker spoke reassuringly and presented programs to fix the wreckage and care for the families of victims. Local, state, and national officials promised a thorough investigation along with all necessary action.

It was a quick fall for the elevator, with lots of wreckage at the bottom. And it's unlikely the crowds will fill elevators so fully again for at least thirty years, when the fall is only a distant memory for a few old folks.

After the fall of real estate that's going on now, bargains will abound, some of them foreclosure sales, even more as pre- or post-foreclosure sales or as short sales. The following chapters examine how to make good real estate purchases of foreclosure properties, as well as excellent real estate sales decisions or decisions to stand pat.

CHAPTER 4

The Rise and Fall of Subprime Lending

BEFORE WE GET TO the nuts and bolts of buying and selling foreclosed real estate, we should say a few words about subprime lending.

It seemed so easy. It all *looked* so easy, so profitable, such a win-win for everybody. And it seemed that all participants were doing their part in the Great Subprime Lending Boom.

And why not? It looked good for everyone. The few nay-sayers were drowned out by the rushing sounds of new money.

It took a bright bunch of people to first conceive of, then seriously plan and release this river of money. The rush of funds went from eager investor to eager Wall Street firm to either one of the many newly created wholesale subprime mortgage firms or to existing wholesale mortgage firms. It then went to local lenders and finally to a group of eager and often first-time borrowers who gladly agreed to repay their loans.

Who Were Subprime Borrowers?

Actually, almost anyone might have fallen into the subprime borrower category.

For example, the subprime borrower could be an applicant with good credit, good employment, and a personal or cultural distrust of banking, whose down-payment funds were not adequately "seasoned"—that is, they had not been banked long enough for traditional underwriting to count them as the borrower's funds. (Lenders call this *mattress money.*)

The subprime borrower could be a plumber buying his second or third fixer-upper who had borrowed enough on the other properties—which were not yet rented—so that his qualifying ratios were out of whack, despite excellent credit, solid employment, and plenty of real estate equity.

The subprime borrower could be the dentist whose tax returns were on extension with a slow-moving accountant, so it was simply more convenient to accept the terms of a subprime loan than to wait for the accountant and also to have to dig out a bunch of bank and investment statements.

The subprime borrower might be the owner of a highly successful business whose track record was simply too short to qualify him for a conventional loan.

The subprime borrower could be an investor who was able to buy properties cheaply because she could do a two-week no-documentation loan through her mortgage broker with less hassle and in less time than it took to borrow from her bank.

The subprime borrower may have been using a short-term subprime loan to avoid private mortgage insurance and still get 90, 95, or 100 percent financing on his real estate purchase.

Regrettably and inexcusably, some subprime borrowers were very marginally qualified or unqualified people placed by financially motivated lenders into loans that they were unable to repay.

And for many people, subprime lending was the alternative to getting no loan and no property at all. Roughly 80 to 90 percent of subprime loans will be repaid as agreed—even in a dramatically different real estate market—with the large majority of those, 80 to 90 percent, being paid off in full within four years.

Subprime mortgages account for a disproportionately high rate of those mortgages made to low, moderate, and financially challenged borrowers. And therein lies the rub: In a poor or flat real estate market, the lenders are unable to recover their loans.

The list of usual main mortgage-default reasons (loss of employment, divorce, illness and large medical or other expenses, death, and disability) can trigger subprime defaults. By their very nature, defaults occur with more frequency among all the subprime borrowers because of one or more of their weaker borrower characteristics.

Many subprime loans required nothing more than the borrower's name, address, social security number, date of birth (a U.S. Homeland Security Department requirement), and a listing of liabilities (loans owed).

There was no request for records of things like employment (even whether or not employed), income, and assets. These were mortgage applications devoid of all the basic types of financial information upon which mortgage loans have traditionally been underwritten.

These "blank applications" for purchase loans up to 90 or 95 percent of the property's purchase price (sometimes called *no-doc* or *true no-doc* loans) did require a credit report. The average U.S. consumer's credit score is about 680. The credit scores required for these blank-application loans generally started at 660 and usually climbed somewhat as the loan-to-value proportion rose toward 95 percent. Refinance true no-doc loans generally went to somewhat lower loan-to-value ratios.

Some of these true no-doc application loans went to strong borrowers: large net-worth individuals with strong investment, retirement, or other income. But others went to borrowers who could qualify for no other type of financing. Some local lenders and borrowers signed on to desperation and "liar" loans, in which the borrower had little or no ability to repay and perhaps, in some small number of exceptional cases, no *intention* of repaying the mortgage loan. Certainly a good chunk of these loans went to borrowers with limited or questionable ability to repay.

Some reduced documentation loans and blank application/no-doc loans were sold and purchased as subprime loans. Some were treated and sold in virtually the same way as they would have been if they had been conventional loans but with a higher interest rate. And some were loans meeting Freddie Mac or Fannie Mae standards for purchase at less than top price.

All these loans were made because funds were made available by a hedge fund or institutional investor looking for higher yields, which bought these loans or a mortgage-backed security based on them as high yield investments. The mortgage-backed securities were rated as investment grade by a credit rating agency, such as Standard & Poor's or Moody's. They were sold by Wall Street firms, which acted solely as sales agent or actually first purchased the mortgage loans from wholesale mortgage lenders, some of them subprime specialty lenders, others full-line wholesale mortgage lenders, or large bank mortgage companies. The Wall Street firms assembled the mortgages into saleable bond-like mortgage-backed securities. The wholesale or wholesale subprime lender or large bank mortgage company paid local lenders for making these loans, funding them "at the table" (or bought them after local lenders closed the loans first using their own funds). The local lenders made the loans to borrowers happy to have a loan for which they could meet the qualifying criteria and were willing to pay a higher interest rate than a rate on conventional loans.

This might sound complicated. The important thing to understand is how dependent each part of the process was on the other.

Reduced-Doc Loans

There were at least two other types of reduced-documentation (reduced-doc) loans:

1. Stated income/stated asset loans: The application showed both income and assets. Assets were not verified, income was not verified, and employment often was verified over the telephone or with a copy of the borrower's business license or a CPA letter verifying self-employment if the borrower was self-employed. These loans usually required two years of self-employment with the same business.
2. No ratio/verified assets loans showed employment and assets on the application but no income. Employment (but not income) was verified as above. Assets were verified, and credit score standards applied.

Many subprime loans are full documentation loans. These are loans with fully documented income and asset requirements (sometimes underwritten by local or wholesale lenders' underwriters to painful paper documentation requirements).

Needless to say, a weak loan with perfect paper documentation is still a much weaker loan than a more loosely documented loan with strong borrower and property characteristics. But as in many other areas of business, that isn't necessarily how the game is played. For example, interest rates oftentimes had the most influence on loan pricing and on the eagerness of loan buyers (investors) and their willingness to buy. This same kind of statement has been accurate in the past with other types of investments and will undoubtedly again prove correct in future decades as to still other investment types.

In an examination of how subprime loans were (and are) made, what is striking is the number of institutions—by type, number, reputation, and investor appeal—that had the chance to say, "Thanks, but no" to the loans. Yet the power of the real estate boom drove lenders to make irrational decisions.

Were Wall Street, credit rating agencies, mortgage firms, and wholesale and local lenders selling loans to institutions that were unaware of the risks? Hardly.

All players in this game had chances to sense the wind before the edge of the storm caught them. As real estate investors look ahead at the residential real estate sector of the U.S. economy, they can't forget that the wind, the tide, the slope of the hill, the direction of the light puff of air on a summer day, and the path of the tornado all take their direction from the short-term interest rate moves of the Fed Open Market Committee *and* from the direction that investors as a group think those rates are going. (Remember that hugely powerful collective wisdom.)

In past months, you have heard from many commentators and even from people in other roles that markets need to adjust. You've also heard that pain and loss are correcting, good, cleansing, and necessary ways of punishing the foolish risk-taker, and that loss and pain miss the wise and diligent.

It may be that only those without family, friends, colleagues, or neighbors in another state now want to say those words. Because this time, many people have known the deep chill and pain of substantial economic loss.

CHAPTER 5

How Foreclosures Happen

NOW THAT THE DISCUSSION of foreclosures has been put into context and you've seen where the current crisis in the housing market comes from and why, it's time to jump into the practical side of things: how you can buy foreclosed property. The first step is to understand what foreclosure is and how it happens.

The word *foreclosure* means "to stop" or "to prevent." Today, we are familiar with the word primarily because of its use in reference to mortgages. In law, to foreclose a mortgage means to cut off a borrower (also called a "mortgagor") from the right to redeem a property. Foreclosure provides the legal means by which a property owner may be stripped of that property because of failure to live up to the terms of the contract made when money was borrowed and real estate pledged as security for the loan.

Now then—a word about lenders and mortgages. Lenders do not give mortgages. This is surprising to many, but it is true.

Lenders loan money. They take back mortgages as security for the loan. Thus, if friends tell you they "got a mortgage" from XYZ mortgage company, they are using accepted parlance to describe the exchange that has taken place, but they are not quite correct. This is an important point to bear in mind for reasons that will become clear.

Purchase-money mortgages are usually signed at a closing, where the seller simultaneously gives a deed to the purchaser. At that time, the purchaser executes loan papers (note and other disclosures) that are given to the lender, as well as a mortgage and other recordable forms (often tax forms), which are likewise given by the closer (along with the deed) to the title company. The title company sees that the mortgage, deed, and other recordable forms are recorded in the local public office that handles real estate recordings. In many locales, title insurance firms or their agencies handle closings directly.

The party doing the mortgaging or pledging is the new owner and in this instance becomes the mortgagor. The lender, which is the party to which the property is pledged, becomes the mortgagee.

Many of the words used in real estate practice have their roots in English law, which in turn was based on Roman law. In such words, most of which are Latin in origin, the suffix "–or" denotes a person performing an action; "–ee" refers to the person receiving the action. Hence, such terms as mortgagor/mortgagee, grantor/grantee, offeror/offeree and so on are common in real estate practice. This discussion uses the terms *mortgagors* and *mortgagees* often and we offer this brief summary to be of help.

Although the underlying principles extend back to English common law, today's foreclosure procedures are governed by state, county, and even local laws and ordinances and practices. There is no national code for foreclosures. If you contemplate buying at foreclosure sales or have other roles relative to foreclosed real estate, there is no substitute for knowing local governing law and procedures. This book outlines the procedures of a large number of localities but there can be—and are—many local variations.

Excellent sources of information include the following:

- Local attorneys and title insurance companies
- Real estate brokers
- Clerk-of-court personnel

- Law firms specializing in foreclosures
- Local lenders and their foreclosure and property disposition specialists
- National lenders and their foreclosure and property disposition specialists
- Firms that specialize in these functions for small- and large-volume lenders and the real estate firms that sell foreclosed real estate for them
- Trustees in bankruptcy and their staffs

Acquiring this knowledge need not take the kind of time or perseverance required to complete a graduate school course, but good tracking and questioning skills definitely help. So does being aware of the natural human tendency to want to appear knowledgeable, the tendency people often have to sometimes be too confident in their own knowledge, and the common inclination to minimize the real expertise of others.

Making Sense of the Terminology

In some states there are mortgages. In others, there are deeds of trust. A deed of trust differs from a mortgage in that the trustor (borrower) signs a deed (subject to conditions) giving legal title in the property to a trustee, who is the actual legal titleholder for the duration of the debt obligation. This practice gives legal title of the property to a third party, the trustee, to assure repayment of the debt obligation.

The deed of trust can facilitate foreclosure. A third-party titleholder is already appointed.

If the borrower is threatened with foreclosure, he can exercise his right of redemption to end the foreclosure proceedings. He can do this either by paying all delinquent obligations, fees, legal expenses, and funds advanced to preserve and protect the real estate collateral (bringing the loan current) or by paying in full the total outstanding debt, fees, legal expenses, and funds advanced. If redemption requirements are not met at some point in the foreclosure proceeding, the right of redemption is ended.

Foreclosure proceedings can last from a handful of months to well over a year if a deficiency judgment (a money judgment against the borrower that survives the foreclosure of the real estate) is sought by the lender, depending on the state or locale in which the property is located.

In the words of the Music Man, you gotta know the territory—foreclosure practice in the jurisdiction in which you wish to acquire foreclosed property—before you can make wise decisions about foreclosed or other real estate in your area.

The most widely used mortgage form in residential real estate lending is the FNMA/FHLMC Uniform Instrument. It is this and like forms that grant foreclosure rights to the lender in the event of default on the underlying debt obligation.

There are five covenants in the mortgage instrument:

1. The mortgagor promises to pay the underlying loan.
2. The mortgagor promises to keep the real estate building(s) insured against fire and other loss for the benefit of the mortgagee.
3. The mortgagor agrees that no buildings will be demolished or removed without the consent of the mortgagee.
4. The mortgagor agrees that the entire principal will become due in the event of default.
5. The mortgagor consents to the appointment of a receiver in the event of default.

All of these provisions grant strong lender rights. For example, the absence of the fourth covenant would mean lenders would only have the rights to bring suit for successive missed payments and not to pursue the full remedy of foreclosure in the event of default.

Short Sales

The heart of a short sale is convincing the lender to accept less than the lender is owed on the loan. The lender further agrees to satisfy (release) the mortgage, and waive any future action against the borrower.

Chapter 13 provides a detailed explanation of this concept, along with a description of the growing use of short sales. In the event of a successful short sale, a mortgagor who is underwater (that is, a borrower who owes more debt than the underlying value of the mortgaged property and has no outside source of funds to restore the loan to current status) may still receive funds from a short sale buyer and actually walk away from a seemingly impossible situation with money and without the credit blemish and pain of a completed foreclosure.

Regardless of your relationship to real estate, an understanding of the concept of short sales is essential. It is one of the most dynamic aspects of what is going on in the real estate marketplace. With a little background knowledge, it is possible to learn how short sales make things in the marketplace both better and worse than they would otherwise appear.

Other Borrower Options

If we didn't know about short sales or other options a borrower has, we might assume that someone facing foreclosure could only sit back and let the inevitable occur. In fact, that borrower has at least three additional options to consider:

1. Sale of the subject property: This requires actual equity in the property (that is, value higher than debt, accrued interest, expenses, and legal and other fees). It also requires the ability to be fleet of foot, the willingness to quickly

retain a real estate agent for quick sale, and the willingness to maintain the property in saleable condition. In some instances, a borrower will pay additional money for a sale to occur, thus "feeding the transaction" but at least getting out from under the mortgage.

2. Deed in lieu of foreclosure: Another option is giving a deed in lieu of foreclosure to the lender, thereby avoiding the pain and credit damage of an actual foreclosure. It's basically a decision by the borrower to give a deed for the mortgaged property to the lender to exit the lending contract—the mortgage loan—as gracefully and with as little damage as possible. It may not be the best of all possible options, but it may be the best option available.

3. Other arrangements: Other factors, including economic and regulatory issues facing lenders, as well as the expenses, delays, and uncertain final outcome of a foreclosure, may induce lenders to offer a struggling borrower a loan restructure or forbearance arrangement on surprisingly favorable terms. Such arrangements will be widely used as lenders' foreclosure options lose appeal in a sideways or declining real estate market.

In the gathering storm of foreclosures, borrowers (and their attorneys and other advisors) and lenders (and their business and foreclosure attorneys, as well as their property management and property sales departments or brokers) will probably find themselves cooperating in some seemingly unlikely combinations of these options. Most of these combinations will benefit both the lender and the borrower. Most will also benefit the communities in which the properties are located. But some borrowers will be unwilling or unable to fully comply with the terms of these agreements.

In traditional foreclosure practice—and assuming borrower workout options were either not attempted, not agreed upon, or ultimately proven unworkable—a foreclosure sale and often a confirmation-of-sale proceeding occur. In some jurisdictions, foreclosure sales are attorney or trustee conducted. In many jurisdictions, a public official—often a sheriff or deputy sheriff—conducts the foreclosure sale.

Foreclosure sales and post-sale confirmation of sale proceedings generally end skirmishes over legal title to the property and the redemption rights of the borrower.

New real estate market conditions and an unprecedented flood of actual and potential foreclosures open options for the creative, thoughtful, well-advised, and swift investor to structure rewarding acquisitions. And there will be more options for borrowers facing the misfortune of a pending or prospective foreclosure.

CHAPTER 6

Payment Option Loans and Other Loan Types

AT THE SAME TIME that subprime, reduced-doc, and no-doc loans became increasingly available, there were and are other types of mortgage loans.

These new types of loans came with benefits as well as with potential problems. The loans arose under various labels, some even under proprietary trade names, but they all offered new benefits for the borrower.

One of the new types of mortgage loan, which attracted a lot of borrower attention and became very popular in many high-priced real estate areas, was a loan with monthly payment amount choices or options that the borrower could select. For the first time in a widely available mortgage product, consumers could select from a number of monthly payment amounts and each following month have the same choice of payment amount, at least for a number of years.

The industry and financial press called these types of loans payment option loans. Typically, the loans were thirty-year loans, and payment options generally included the following choices:

1. **The lowest payment option:** Usually, this consisted of a very low monthly payment determined by a formula but

still satisfying the terms of the loan. This payment option was available to the borrower for a number of years—say, the first five years of the loan term—after which larger catch-up payments were required.

2. **Interest only on the outstanding principal balance:** Again, this option was available for a certain period of the loan term, after which the borrower was required to make larger catch-up payments.

3. **Regular amortizing payment:** This is the monthly amount calculated to pay off the loan at the end of its term in years. This is the type of mortgage and payment on a thirty-year fixed-rate loan that most consumers are familiar with.

4. **Higher payment:** If made regularly and on time, this option would allow a borrower to totally pay off the loan balance in a shorter number of years than the full term of the loan. Lenders offered ten-, fifteen-, twenty-, or twenty-five-year payment options. On payment option loans with a pre-payment penalty, this is actually more restrictive than a standard or regular fixed-rate loan without pre-payment penalty.

Some payment option loans were fixed rate. With others, the interest rate was adjustable.

Here are the central characteristics of payment option loans:

- They have interest rates higher than fixed-rate conventional loans (the tradeoff for the payment option feature).
- If the lowest monthly payment is selected, the loan balance increases each time the lowest payment is made. This is growing loan principal or *negative amortization,* and it's why the catch-up payments may start earlier than under the interest-only option.

- These loans can seem to make sense in an appreciating or rapidly appreciating real estate market. If the lowest payment only is made in a flat or declining market, equity can be quickly eaten up. In fact, the borrower can end up upside-down (owing more than current market value of the property).
- The lowest monthly payment option is an artificially low amount. Its purpose is to appeal to the consumer. (It's usually computed by a simple formula so that local lenders can compute an actual monthly payment figure to sell to prospective borrowers.)

These loan types have built-in features that can lull the consumer into what can later become a very challenging or untenable position. In the declining real estate market of many cities, these loans can be very problematic.

Many readers are familiar with adjustable rate mortgages (ARMs), which have been around for a long time. Just a few words about them: A typical ARM loan has a fixed low interest rate for a given number of years. Typically, the initial rate is set for one, two, three, or five years. After that, it adjusts annually based on a formula set forth in the loan documents.

- Many lenders call the initial rate for the initial period a *teaser rate*. It is an artificially low rate whose purpose is to tease or entice the consumer to take the loan.
- Adjustable mortgages make sense in some limited circumstances, such as if you're given a two-year job assignment somewhere and you know your employer will transfer you to another state at the end of your assignment.
- After the initial period of the teaser rate, an index-plus-margin formula applies. It is higher than the then-available fixed rates.
- In a flat or declining real estate market, adjustable rate loans can be very problematic.

Forty-year fixed-rate loans became widely available in 2005 or so. Their purpose was to provide some payment relief to borrowers. Here are a few words about this little-used loan product:

- Interest rates are somewhat higher than on thirty-year fixed-rate loans.
- The amount of payment relief to the consumer is very small.

Alt-A Loans

Alt-A is the name given to another type of loan for borrowers who fall just below the criteria for becoming a prime Fannie Mae or Freddie Mac conforming borrower. One characteristic necessary for approving the loan (or more than one) may be lower than on prime loans.

For example, the borrower's credit score might be twenty, thirty, or forty points or more lower than that required for a prime loan, but he or she could still be approved for an Alt-A loan. Loan pricing for these loans is lower and, accordingly, the consumer interest rate is somewhat higher than for a prime loan.

This type of loan has been widely available since 2002 or so. It was a major break for those borrowers whose credit history was just shy of the mark. Alt-A loans likewise became readily available and marketable through the same sources for funding as conventional loans. Alt-A loans funded many first-time buyers who previously couldn't buy at all, and they were a factor in increased demand for starter and move-up properties.

Along with the new or increased usage of all the available mortgage options, millions of people were able to purchase the homes of their dreams. Almost all of them would have been well-performing borrowers had a perfect storm not come their way.

CHAPTER 7

The Best Mortgage Loan and the Second-Best Mortgage Loan

THE BEST MORTGAGE LOAN is no mortgage loan. These may be surprising words, given that they come from a real estate broker and a mortgage lender. Most mortgage loans make real estate sales possible, and they are the bread and butter for any mortgage lender. But we know how correct those words are.

This isn't the first time you will come across words of warning about the risks of highly leveraged borrowing (high-loan-to-value loans). The great exception is buying a well-priced property to occupy as a primary residence along with the willingness to live frugally and personally do much of the home improvement work.

The next best real estate loan under any real estate circumstance is a fixed-rate long-term loan with moderate closing costs.

High closing costs dramatically increase the true total cost of a mortgage loan if it is repaid in one, two, or three years, and it's much worse if it's paid off sooner. It's hugely worse if it is paid off early and also contains a pre-payment penalty. Thus, it is almost always better to focus on closing costs, fixed-rate terms, and absence of pre-payment penalty than to focus on interest rate.

Some lenders take advantage of the consumer tendency to focus on interest rate. They advertise then try to direct borrowers to a loan with a low appearing rate and high closing costs. It is almost invariably a far worse choice for the consumer. Let's investigate why that is.

Most mortgage loans are paid off long before the term is up. Most mortgage loans have a relatively long term of ten, fifteen, twenty, or thirty years, even if they are adjustable and the rate moves sharply higher after the initial fixed-rate.

The reasons for the mortgage payoff early are many. Here they are, in no particular order:

- Sale of property: This may be triggered by a number of factors, including an employment transfer; the need to downsize; increase or reduction in family size, death, disability, or relocation to elderly housing; retirement move; the desire for another property; a move to a larger home.
- Refinance of the property: This may be triggered by some of the above reasons, as well as a need for additional funds for a broad range of purposes, including college expenses; repayment of other non–tax-deductible debt; home improvement or addition; general living expenses; investment or business purposes; or to buy a second home or recreational property. Some refinances are driven by lower interest rates, which make a refinance advantageous (particularly if closing costs are low or zero).
- Early repayment of a mortgage

A mortgage company belonging to one of the authors has refinanced thousands of clients with total closing costs ranging from $900 to nothing down. These clients typically paid an interest rate generally one-eighth or one-quarter percent higher than borrowers at other firms with much higher closing costs and saved dramatically when the loans paid off early. Closing costs generally don't become tax deductible for most people, and interest paid generally is. With early payoff or multiple loans, those low or nonexistent closing costs saved customers thousands of dollars.

Some borrowers refinance because of a need for a lower monthly payment amount, perhaps refinancing from a fifteen-year to a thirty-year term, even at a slightly higher interest rate, for a lower monthly payment.

A loan may pay off early for any of these reasons and many more.

CHAPTER 8

Other Reasons for Foreclosure

BESIDES SIMPLE DEFAULT on a loan, there are other reasons for properties to go into foreclosure—for example, because of nonpayment of back taxes. Occasionally, you may read in your local paper about public sale of tax liens or tax sales. Real estate taxes take precedence over all other claims, including those of any mortgage.

Some background on this type of foreclosure is probably in order. Prior to World War II, lenders took payments of principal and interest only; mortgagors were permitted to make tax payments directly to the municipality. One of the main reasons this practice was permitted was the fact that the ratio of debt to value in those days was usually quite low.

If the lender had to foreclose and pay up back taxes, the value of the property was sufficient to cover all obligations.

With the advent of the Federal Housing Administration and the provisions of the Servicemen's Readjustment Act of 1944, however, low-equity mortgage situations became more common. The VA guaranteed a mortgage for 100 percent of the purchase price and thus made it possible for homes to be bought for no cash down. So lenders were willing to make those loans. The FHA administered a low-cash-down-payment loan guarantee program for nonveterans, requiring as little as 3 percent down payment. Private mortgage insurance (PMI) firms appeared on the scene to add further lender comfort to making low-down-payment loans.

Lenders became concerned about the prospect of purchasers failing to make tax and insurance payments when due. Under previous arrangements, taxing authorities could have taken over the property in such cases, mortgage or no mortgage, maybe without notice to the lender if the borrower was neglecting only tax payments.

To protect lenders, tax escrows (and often homeowner's insurance escrows as well) were required. Taxes and insurance would be prepaid to the lender, into an escrow account, as part of the monthly mortgage payment. The lender would then pay taxes and insurance when due. It was a fine setup that brought a measure of discipline to the process, and the same procedure was eventually applied to conventional as well as government-backed loans.

Most lenders require that escrow accounts be established with the lender for the purpose of making sure that taxes are paid on time and that homeowner's insurance is continually in force, on at least all low-down-payment loans. Hence, many monthly mortgage payments include one-twelfth of annual taxes, and sometimes also one-twelfth of annual homeowner's insurance premiums, as part of the "regular" amount.

Almost all escrow accounts also have a cushion or reserve to cover tax increases or insurance premium increases. Some lenders became overzealous in collecting escrows, and federal regulations now limit the amount of escrow funds that can be collected. A down payment of 20 percent (or 20 percent equity, on refinance loans) has become the standard requirement for waiving tax and insurance escrows if lenders permit waiver. Subprime (nonconventional) lending is often a surprising exception to this general requirement. Logic would suggest that lenders would require tax and insurance escrows on subprime loans. They do not.

Tax Sales

Most tax sales don't originate with properties that are mortgaged. Curiously, they take place on properties that are usually free and clear of mortgages. This is not so difficult to understand, given the requirement for tax and insurance escrows on many mortgages. Escrows or lender verification that taxes and insurance have been paid is a vital part of most mortgage loan servicing.

Who, then, defaults because of problems with tax payments? In many cases, it's senior citizens who simply don't understand their obligations, as other capabilities diminish.

Often, a borrower dies, and the spouse or other parties in the household become unable to cope with business matters. A notice arrives in the mail; it is ignored. Unpaid tax bills grow. The legal machinery starts to move and cranks onward slowly. The owner may assume things have blown over. He or she may have more pressing matters, or may act as if other matters are more important. Finally the property is "sold for back taxes," with the owner often the last person to know. Sadly, no one in the owner's circle of friends, family, or advisors may have been able or available to make clear the gravity of the situation.

In such an unfortunate (but not that uncommon) case, the system progresses regardless of the state of knowledge of the homeowner. These tax sales (and sheriff's sales, for other delinquent obligations that are examined on page 44) differ from the standard lender foreclosure sale in that there are often homestead exemptions and different redemption periods involved.

Let's look at the mechanics of a tax sale. When the municipality puts tax liens up for sale (and that's technically what is going on in some jurisdictions), that taxing authority (usually the county) is in effect selling a debt obligation with its attached rights, a concept that sounds strange indeed.

Depending on the law in a particular jurisdiction, the party who buys the claim has the right to claim title to the property after expiration of the statutory time for redemption. That period could be perhaps one or two years or more, depending on local law.

During the redemption period, interest is accruing at an interest rate permitted under the statute. In some states the redemption period has already lapsed by the time of tax sale. Local practice varies substantially.

A bit of tax sale history and a local legend are in order. In the 1800s and early 1900s, when land was being timbered in many parts of this country, a large amount of logged-off forest land was simply abandoned by owners who considered it worthless or virtually worthless after timbering.

Thus, huge amounts of land were taken to tax sale by the taxing authority for back unpaid taxes, often by statute the local county. Much of this land was purchased by private parties at the tax sale auction. And much of this land was purchased at tax sale auction by the county (no bidders) and then subsequently sold to private parties.

Much of the no-bid land that went to counties was retained by them and became part of public land in this country. You'd be surprised how much land, now prime recreational or second-home property, has such a tax sale history.

One now stunningly gorgeous parcel on the shores of Lake Superior, totally breathtaking in its beauty and scope, is simply one (large) example of countless thousands of parcels across our land with a logging and tax sale history. The same history applies to vast amounts of farming acreage and urban parcels in the years of and following the Great Depression.

In addition, property abandonment or simple neglect to pay taxes has always been and is still alive and well. You would be surprised at the amount of land that's in economically depressed urban or remote areas of your state or an adjoining state that goes to tax sale. Out-of-state owners, owners who become disabled or financially distressed, or owners who simply become too busy to deal anymore with a distant asset they consider to be of low value or too much bother to deal with routinely allow properties to go to tax sale.

Not everyone is watching every delinquent tax sale everywhere all the time. Not every property that goes to tax sale, in effect a foreclosure for prior years' taxes, may be an island in Sturgeon Bay, Wisconsin, with two houses on it, but you'd be surprised at the opportunities that crop up.

The late-night infomercials are definitely not all hype. Remember, someone's economic backwater, where most tax sales occur, may be someone else's idea of a neat little place in the country or of a great opportunity to get an early start in a revitalization area with great prospects.

Remember, like lender foreclosures, what happens at tax sales or tax foreclosures varies with jurisdiction and local practice. Because many parcels are virtually worthless or a liability negative, success in a tax sale depends upon strong information-gathering skills, diligence, and planning. It's a lot to hope for that one day you might be paying a speeding ticket in the courthouse, your pockets filled with plenty of money, and as you start to walk out, you come upon a tax sale about to start up with just the perfect property available and no other buyers in sight. That would be a lucky day indeed, but you're much more likely to create your own good luck with some research and forethought.

Sheriff's Sales

Recovery by a creditor for obligations other than a mortgage default is usually carried out by means of a sheriff's sale. In these actions there are other considerations and regulations that enter into the process. It is necessary to stress here once again that there is no federal law on these subjects. Instead, state and local law govern. Get all the information you can, and double- and triple-check it.

Many states and municipalities have homestead exemptions, which apply in sheriff's sales for judgments other than mortgage debt. The exemption is usually expressed in dollar amounts, which vary by state statute. What this means is that if you acquire a property under this type of sale, you must give an allowance of the homestead exemption amount to the foreclosed party.

Why is such a measure necessary? There were once some people who abused the system, buying up judgments from creditors and foreclosing mercilessly on unfortunate owners. The homestead exemption is one small window of protection for the homeowner. Without it, many victimized homeowners would be destitute.

In addition, you should know that foreclosure actions for other obligations by sheriff's sale may differ from customary mortgage foreclosures in that they may carry with them a right of redemption. Or at least they may be treated differently by local judges. The period in which the defaulting party has the opportunity to make restitution is generally identified by statute, and in practice, the local judges often call the shots. Such things may be some protection from foreclosure for nonmortgage debt, particularly if the debt is small. Still, a bunch of these judgment sales occur to satisfy creditor judgments even though the creditor initially had no mortgage.

Nonmonetary Reasons for Default

Foreclosure actions can be instituted for nonmonetary reasons, too, although this is far less frequent than monetary default. The trick is to remember that the mortgage agreement is a contract; when the contract is breached, the borrower can't rewrite what was agreed to according to what the borrower believes the conditions should be. If the borrower breaks the mortgage agreement, there may be some unpleasant consequences. Examples of what could trigger a lender decision to foreclose could be deliberate destruction of some of the improvements on the property or gross neglect of the property, even though payments are still being made.

One of the most common nonmonetary reasons for default and the right to foreclose is the sale of the property to a third party when the property is subject to an existing mortgage that is nonassumable and "due on sale." In simpler terms, a lender can declare a default if the borrower sells the property and tries to avoid paying the "due on sale" mortgage. The new buyer could and will face a foreclosure.

The mortgage must be paid up. The remedy for breach is foreclosure. You can be sure title companies or attorneys weren't consulted on these "sales."

There are other reasons for nonmonetary actions by the mortgagee, including breach of other covenants and restrictions contained in the mortgage. When these conditions exist, the mortgagee has the right to accelerate the payments—in other words, call for payment of the entire principal balance, even though all the monthly payments have been made.

In these instances, the payment history is not at issue; the nonmonetary violations are of such a nature that the mortgagee wants out. The option of making payments on a monthly basis can be revoked if the lender, in protecting the mortgaged property, chooses to foreclose.

CHAPTER 9

Deed in Lieu of Foreclosure

WHAT ABOUT OTHER PEOPLE who are facing a foreclosure of their property—for example, people who are changing employment and need to move to another locality, maybe many states away? In the case of a corporate job transfer, there is usually no problem. The employer will buy the home at a predetermined figure. The company will then continue the sale and will be responsible for the care in the event of vacancy. But not all job moves are with the same employer.

Sometimes the people are doing it on their own. They have been offered a better position elsewhere, current employment has ended involuntarily, but the responsibility of the move is completely theirs. High on the list of things to be done is the sale of the present home.

It is possible an out-of-town move has already been made and the home is already on the market. Now, several months later, the borrower/owner finds that a sale at the figure needed is out of sight. Nothing in the neighborhood is moving. The price likely to be offered might not even cover the mortgage.

In addition, there is a real estate broker commission to be paid as well as other expenses associated with the sale, costs that will force the borrower/owner to dip into his or her small savings, already stretched to the maximum to cover the costs of transfer. Alternately, savings may already be exhausted.

Some borrowers making a move like this may be able to borrow and pay money so that the upside-down sale can occur. But many, maybe most, will find it beyond their ability to handle this stressful situation.

Looks hopeless, doesn't it? What should the mortgagors do? Call in a mover for the remaining furniture and drift off into the night and let the lender foreclose? That might appear to be a solution, but as the lender notices pile up and the foreclosure begins, the homeowner's credit rating suffers.

Well, how about renting the property? That might be a temporary solution. But what if a good tenant loses employment or gets sick and cannot make rent payments? This happens. Renters' credit patterns are usually not as secure as those of homeowners. And the problem becomes even bigger if the owner is in some other part of the country than the property, trying to deal with a bank that wants its mortgage payments.

That's just one scenario. There are many other ways in which this financial bind can happen. The borrower didn't buy the house to rent. The borrower bought it to occupy. At this point in these situations, equity in the property may be very little or nil. The borrower's credit has been good, all bills have been paid, and there are no judgments or legal proceedings pending.

If the borrower walks away from the property and leaves the path open for the lender to commence the foreclosure proceedings, the lender has also been given a large burden. The burden is the foreclosure procedure, which requires time and money and carries risks and uncertainties.

For example, the lender now has an empty house that it must protect. If it does not, the house could be stripped and further vandalized resulting in untold repairs, replacements, and expenses. Under these circumstances, the borrower could offer or the lender could ask for a deed in lieu of foreclosure.

A deed in lieu of foreclosure is the transfer to the property to the lender "as is" instead of foreclosure.

The lender is not required to accept a deed in any of these circumstances, but what are the alternatives if it does not? Either way, it is going to have an empty house to add to its inventory with all of the problems that attend such circumstances.

Beginning foreclosure proceedings also delays the sale of the house to a new owner. The lender will have to serve the defaulting party with court papers. All this incurs time, marketing expenses, carrying costs, damage exposure, and uncertainty. From the lender's standpoint, deed in lieu of foreclosure can be a good alternative.

The lender will want to know first if there are any liens against the property. The lender will conduct a search of all the public records. Next, the lender will conduct both a property title search by a title insurance company and get a credit report on the borrower. It may also require a current borrower financial statement. If all these are favorable and there are no problems, it may agree to accept a deed in lieu of foreclosure.

Often in these situations lenders require an additional legal document called a Deed in Lieu of Foreclosure Agreement. Borrowers should retain legal counsel to review this document for reasons including tax implications (which may be very ugly). At this point a borrower's attorney may be able to negotiate additional favorable conditions for the borrower. Lenders will likewise want to make sure all the legal loose ends are wrapped up so there is no subsequent challenge.

This brings us to the purpose of introducing this process in a book on foreclosures. After all, the property was not foreclosed, but now it is a part of the lender's owned real estate.

Now the lender is in the position you were in when you owned the property. It has a property to sell. It has to get rid of it. The property has to be reduced to money, the commodity of lender commerce. There are plenty of lender incentives to sell and usually few if any incentives to retain the property, even for a short while.

Lenders are accustomed to quickly selling real estate in these circumstances. They usually have no trouble in adjusting to the current market conditions. They probably will sell the property for less than the mortgage balance, often considerably less.

A new buyer could not have gotten this deal from the former homeowner, and the homeowner could not have closed on it. The borrower could not do it because the outstanding mortgage would have to be satisfied before the borrower could convey clear title. But now, with the deed in lieu of foreclosure, the lender can and does sell. That is why we advise all persons who are looking to buy foreclosures to also contact lenders, which may mean their property management unit or contractor and/or the real estate broker who handles sales of the properties they have acquired. Some of the best opportunities for a great buy are from the lender's inventory.

If you are creditworthy, and you can close the purchase quickly, the lender may be very happy to deal with you. Lenders getting rid of properties (and that's how they think of it) want cash offers and quick closings. There is some chance you might even be offered a very favorable mortgage loan as well.

There are many success stories about purchases from lenders who have foreclosed or accepted a deed in lieu of foreclosure. We urge you to talk with lenders. There are plenty of good deals to be had directly from lenders and whoever handles their properties after they take title. Finding the right party to first speak and then negotiate with is a major challenge. In most cases, the lender has probably delegated the sale of acquired property to a management or real estate firm. Learning which firms sell lender-acquired property can give you very valuable information. Much work and persistence may be needed. Good tracking skills are important and are often necessary to learn which properties are lender-owned. Foreclosure law firms can be an excellent information source.

At the foreclosure auction sale, bidders generally do not know what is in the house. When the lender owns it, after foreclosing or taking a deed in lieu of foreclosure, the property can usually be inspected. Bring a real estate–savvy friend, broker, inspector, and contractor, or as many of them as you can get together along with you for an inspection. Some of these people may need to come separately, because of busy schedules.

Homes taken by deed in lieu of foreclosure are often the better homes in a lender's inventory because the former owners did not lose the home in a painful foreclosure. They may have taken excellent care of the property until their hand was forced.

PART TWO

How to Buy Foreclosed and Distressed Properties

CHAPTER 10

You Have to Know
the Numbers

THROUGHOUT THIS BOOK, we pound on these statements: You have to know the territory, and you have to know the numbers. So how do you learn the numbers?

First, let's take a look at appraisals. We know appraisals can be a bit tedious, and they cost money—about $400 per appraisal. This is an amount that many people do not want to spend. Who would want to spend money for an appraisal on a property they might not even buy? Nonetheless, we recommend it if the lender owning the property will permit access to an appraiser. Even an exterior-only appraisal, which usually costs less, is very valuable to you.

An appraisal takes the form of a written document on a standard form called the Uniform Residential Appraisal Report, six pages long. Almost every detail about a property is there on the form. On the second page, the form lists the subject property, then lists three comparable properties that have recently sold. Each comparable is adjusted up or down in dollar amount as compared to the subject property components.

For example, if the subject property has one bath, and the second has one and a half baths, the appraiser makes an adjustment to offset the half bath. At the end of the report the appraiser determines a value by these adjustments. In other words, an appraisal is an expert opinion of value prepared by a licensed and certified appraiser and is generally prepared for a lender to be certain the property is worth financing. Appraisals also may be ordered by a probate court or by individuals wanting to know what their property is worth. As you'll see, very few sellers really want to know what their property is worth.

Most sellers use another way to get an estimate of what their property is worth. It is called a market analysis. All residential real estate agents do market analyses routinely. They pull three or four comparable properties from the Multiple Listing Service and do their own unofficial appraisal. (MLS is the information system typically owned by the real estate firms or their association. It gathers and provides members with sales price and listing prices on properties in their area.) This report is not considered to be an expert appraisal for a lender or anyone else—it is an estimate, but an estimate is a way to get numbers. When a market analysis is done for a potential seller, the real estate agent sometimes has a bias toward a higher number to secure the listing. In your discussions with a real estate agent, from time to time you will ask for a market analysis.

Although agents will sometimes perform these analyses for free for clients, if you offer to pay for a market analysis you actually want to buy, the agent is more likely to take you on as a client, since that way she knows she will be paid. But if you put that agent through a lot of time for nothing, you will lose. And you had better believe that agents can spot users.

Another way to do market analysis is to learn the numbers yourself, either by studying real estate appraisal or getting sales prices from a title company. Whichever way you choose, "You gotta know the numbers." Why is that such a big deal?

Here's why. If you don't know the approximate current value and approximate future value of a piece of property, you will never buy anything for fear of making a mistake or, in this case, losing money.

Once you know the numbers, you're ready to consider buying some foreclosed property. To do that, you need to understand exactly how a foreclosure works.

Stages of Foreclosure

An actual foreclosure will have as its first step the filing of foreclosure papers, in which the appropriate public office, usually a court, files a notice of pending legal action—a lis pendens (Latin for "pending legal action")—with the public real estate recordings office and service of a summons on the borrower. (Remember deed-of-trust states and state or local practice can vary at all stages and aspects of a foreclosure.)

The foreclosure action is now a matter of public record.

Word of substantially late mortgage payments may already have been sold by one or more of the credit reporting agencies (or one or more of the national credit repositories) to those who wish to purchase that information.

Ever wonder why you receive highly targeted credit solicitations in the mail from lenders who seem to know a lot about your finances? Many are purchasing highly specific data from the national very-eager-to-sell credit repositories. These targeted data sales may specify, for example, all consumers who have one mortgage only, with credit card balances between specified dollar amounts, in particular states or metropolitan areas or zip codes. Some sales of data are so specific that privacy and proprietary issue challenges to them have already been raised on many fronts.

Local publications may publish notice of foreclosure suits and/or lis pendens filings.

Prior to the commencement of the foreclosure suit, the foreclosing law firm will receive a report from a title insurance company detailing mortgages, tax liens, judgments, and any other matters of record affecting the property. Generally all parties (with the usual exception of the local taxing authorities, whose liens for real estate taxes have priority that cannot be affected by foreclosure) are joined as defendants in the foreclosure action.

They are joined so their interests, mortgage, or other liens (contractor or judgment liens, for example) are extinguished if the foreclosure action is taken all the way to foreclosure sale and sale confirmation.

If the foreclosing party was negligent in notifying junior lien holders, for example those holding a second mortgage, those creditors not joined in the action would have a valid claim against the new owner. Could such a claim affect a purchaser at foreclosure sale or subsequently? Yes! And that's why a title insurance policy is so important to a foreclosure or pre- or post-foreclosure purchaser.

Title insurance letter reports are informational only, modest in price, and provide no or only a very modest amount of indemnity in the case of error or omission. Title insurance policies cost serious money. They provide full purchase-price coverage, backed by the title insurance company's promise to pay and defend any challenges to the title of the property and are ultimately backed by the company's financial reserves.

Is it wise to purchase financially distressed or foreclosed property without an actual title policy? Only if you really know what you are doing, if you don't mind rolling the dice, and you are prepared for the full financial and legal consequences of title surprises.

There must be personal service of the foreclosure summons on the defaulting borrower (by sheriff's deputy or other official or private process servers). As many defaulting borrowers make themselves scarce, the alternative, to personal service of papers is an item in a publication designated for such legal notices.

Many jurisdictions require notice by publication even if there has been personal service of papers. Even if that's not required, foreclosure attorneys regularly do so as a matter of course.

Tenants may or may not have the right to remain in a build-ing being foreclosed. Many leases provide that the premises must be vacated in the event of foreclosure. Some tenants may have rented with an option to purchase and may have paid option money. Their circumstances may complicate the foreclosure pro-cess or options of a purchaser.

We've heard of borrowers or even third parties renting dis-tressed property and pocketing the payments without making payments to the mortgagee. Such occupancy issues can some-times require serious unscrambling.

Foreclosure proceedings may appear straightforward. But often a potential buyer must determine who exactly the foreclos-ing party is: Is the foreclosing lender a first mortgage holder or a subsequent (second or third) mortgage holder? For example, a foreclosing second mortgage lender is doing so subject to the rights of the first mortgage holder. A seemingly low loan amount being foreclosed may appear deceptively inviting. Don't be fooled by the size of the foreclosing mortgage. Second mortgage foreclo-sures, while relatively less frequent, do occur.

Just remember, the obligation to determine what is actually being acquired at foreclosure sale (or pre- or post-foreclosure) is strictly the buyer's. This is just one reason why we think purchas-ing a title insurance policy is absolutely necessary.

CHAPTER 11

Preforeclosure—Contacting Mortgagors Prior to the Sale

LET'S ASSUME THAT YOUR aim is to purchase a home for yourself. If you become aware of someone in financial difficulty in an area where you'd like to live, you might do well to contact the mortgagor directly. By contact directly, we mean just that: Go to the house, knock on the door, and speak to the people face to face. Don't rely on the phone.

The strongest and most effective way to deal with people always has been and always will be personal contact. This is why we are advising you to go straight to the door if you go this route. Let them see you, meet you, and learn that you are not in the business of buying and selling houses, which in insider lingo is called *flipping*. They'll perhaps feel safer dealing with you.

If a lis pendens has been filed, chances are that the mortgagors have been already been contacted by local real estate companies and investors. As someone who wants to buy the home as a residence, you may stand a much better chance than those other potential buyers because homeowners in financial difficulty are likely to feel that the investors and brokers are "out to steal" their home.

After all, an investor or broker speaking to a homeowner is approaching the person on what is basically a "wholesale" purchase.

They will be looking to turn it over for a profit; you, as a buyer for your own residence, will often be prepared to pay a higher price. Your message may have a much easier time getting heard.

How do you find properties that are facing foreclosure?

One way is to go to the county clerk's office and read the postings. Another method is to follow the published notices in the newspapers. If you are interested in a particular location, you'd do well to buy the local paper for official legal notices in that area. If there's a foreclosure in that county, the chances are good that it will be published in the local paper, which carries legal notices. Check with the county clerk's office for the correct paper. When you read the notice in the local paper, it will usually show the name of the lender's attorney. Even here, however, you should be resigned to the fact that many people will not go out of their way to give you information. The reason we propose you call the lender or attorney at all is that someone may know the case well and may be able, and willing, to pass along useful information. There is no substitute for all your own efforts to gather information.

The Internet and More Ways to Locate Foreclosures

The Internet is one more source of foreclosure information and might well be the easiest to use. By searching the word "foreclosures for your state" you will find volumes of leads and links. Of course, the links vary greatly in their usefulness, and many have a fee attached for their information, but that fee may or may not be worth it. RealtyTrac.com provides useful foreclosure statistics.

Here are two more Internet lists well worth studying.

1. **VA Foreclosures:** The Veterans Administration forecloses on their guaranteed loans and places those properties for sale with management/sale brokers around the country.

The list is available online at *www.homesales.gov*, and the properties are all sold by registered real estate agents.

2. **FHA Foreclosures:** Lists of FHA properties are online at *hud.gov/homes* and are sold by registered real estate agents.

In your discussion with a real estate agent of your choosing, be sure to say that you might want to buy a VA or FHA property. Be sure that agent has or will register with the FHA or VA to get a key, and be sure that agent knows the procedure or will learn the procedure and get all the VA forms. The offer to purchase is a national form, not a state approved form. The procedure is a specialty, unlike normal real estate brokerage. Again, prearranged financing or knowing exactly if or how the VA will provide financing is absolutely essential. Some agency properties can be very good buys. Others are real stinkers. Potential buyers can either take out a new mortgage to buy one, or for a small increase in price the agency may finance it.

We have sold many VA properties in the past. We looked at each one in our area that came on the market and picked and chose which ones to sell. Some of those are very good buys, some are not. "You have to know the numbers."

Purchasing properties preforeclosure can make sense if you are organized, well financed, well-advised, and are doing it to buy a property to occupy as your residence. It can also be rewarding as a part-time line of work or full-time endeavor.

Ask a lot of questions at a lot of places and you will find the most productive method to gather the information you are seeking.

Preforeclosure: Locating Borrowers and Properties

Go online and search the terms "before foreclosure" and "pre-foreclosure" statewide, regionally, and locally. You will find much information as well as databases for sale. If you buy such a list from the right firm, it may be a wise purchase. Most experts would certainly recommend you start small with what you buy. As is the case in other fields, some lists will prove quite useful, and others will be almost worthless. Don't be afraid to ask a bunch of questions of the list company, and don't be afraid to check with other sources and do a full due-diligence search before you buy. Have a title company check the title status. Purchasing a list without doing due diligence is not recommended. The Internet is a great blessing with the astounding amount of information available from it. The accompanying curse is that the number of sellers has exploded and the consumer's ability to evaluate the worth of what the sellers are offering is limited. A list sold to several parties will decline in value with each sale and perhaps to the point of being worthless.

Consider placing an ad in a local newspaper: "Facing foreclosure? I buy properties facing foreclosure and pay cash. Call me at this number." Someone in preforeclosure might contact you.

Word-of-mouth contacts, putting out the word through local organizations, banks and finance (second mortgage) lenders, and attorneys, and targeted letters to those likely to come in contact with financially distressed borrowers can prove useful. Most of these people and organizations will need to feel comfortable with your credibility, honesty, and financial capacity. It will take time and effort to get a good reputation in preforeclosure purchases from distressed borrowers.

It gets easier after your first successes.

The Agreement

If you reach a verbal agreement with a mortgagor, and he or she won't use an attorney in finalizing the sale, you must incorporate a clause in your written agreement (and everything must be reduced to a written agreement) stating that you have advised the borrower that he or she should secure the services of counsel, but he or she has chosen not to do so.

Make the letter of agreement as clear as possible; spell everything out in the most detailed and obvious terms. Every component of your agreement must be in layman's language that is impossible to misunderstand, or as close as you can come to that standard. In the event of a later dispute, you will not be able to defend yourself by saying, "I assumed he understood." And people do change their minds.

If you will be accepting payments from the mortgagors and allowing them to remain in the house, for instance, don't write about "foreclosure" or "dispossession." Write, "If you don't make the payments as agreed, I have the right to go to court and have the judge sign an order that will enable me to have you removed from the house. That means the sheriff will put your furniture on the curb and you and your family as well." Blunt? Yes. But you must nevertheless write it in language that anyone will understand, then read it back and ask if it's clear and if there are any questions.

Whether you are going to be an investor or are buying a house for your own occupancy, you should not skimp on legal services. Obtain the services of a competent real estate attorney whose job will be to represent you. You need someone to advise you before, during, and also after your real estate moves. Sadly, and expensively, for those unwilling to retain attorneys before they commit themselves, a lot of legal work is "post-mess." Have and use the benefit of legal advice before you act, or don't plan on having much fun or many successful outcomes.

There are many areas of the country where people skip using lawyers when drafting sale agreements. The authors of this book always recommend using an attorney and use them in our own real estate matters. People who ask whether they really need an attorney for this step bring to mind women who ask whether they really need a doctor when they go into labor. Of course, more than one police officer has delivered a baby, but if a complication arises, you need a competent professional who knows the law and the business. How many people are certain that their situation will be completely free of complications? You never know what will crop up in a real estate transaction. Include the services of an attorney in your cost-of-acquisition figures.

Equity Sharing

One method of home sharing and ownership that is often proposed by late-night infomercials is the "equity sharing" program. In it's simplest terms, this is an agreement between two people to share in the money or labor and to share in the profit. The idea is often advanced as a method for handling the party facing foreclosure. It is a bad idea. If you're going to be sharing a title with people who are constantly in financial hot water, you are asking for trouble.

Any judgments they incur can be attached to the property; that attachment is not in proportion to the other party's ownership. It is completely against the property. Your newfound partner can possibly strip you of all your ownership in the property by, for instance, borrowing from someone else, never repaying the loan, and having the case go to judgment, which attaches to the real estate you share.

Equity share programs are all right in certain circumstances, but they represent a huge no-no when dealing with a party facing foreclosure. These ideas are for people who have good credit records but are low on cash. One very good way is for one party to put up the cash and the other partner to put up the labor, all on a fifty-fifty basis. You can make similar shared-responsibility agreements, but only with someone you know and trust and who has good credit standing.

The hard fact is that there are certain types of people in this world who can't handle money. Property managers have heard all of the hard-luck stories. Many try to compensate by taking an extra month's security deposit from tenants who seem to have a history of financial problems. It rarely works. The tenants will use it up. People who say, "Everything always happens to me!" are usually right.

There is no full precaution you can take against people who are deadbeats. If you must deal with them, do what you have to do and get out of the deal quickly. The longer you work with them, the more it will cost you. Painful experience has shown that these people are constantly in hot water. Even if you solve their immediate problem, they'll be back in trouble next year, next month, and maybe even next week. Unless you're in a completely foolproof position (which is hard to even imagine), don't get involved in a long-term deal. You can empathize all you want—but don't sympathize. You can't afford to take their problems on as your own.

CHAPTER 12

Acquire Knowledge and Avoid Emotional Pitfalls

WE WANTED TO SHARE a hard-won lesson based on our own experience as well as derived from the mistakes we've observed with surprising frequency in the real estate transactions of others.

Here's the single best piece of real estate advice you could listen to when buying: Understand that in the vast majority of cases, real estate is a commodity. There are other three-bedroom ranches, four- and five-bedroom colonials, two- and four-family rental properties, farmettes, and usually even other "estate" type properties in a given market. Don't get so emotionally attached to one property that it blinds you to others.

Time and again we have seen purchasers with hearts set on a particular property whose hope to buy that property fails for one of the many reasons real estate transactions don't go together:

- The sellers have already accepted another offer.
- The property inspection shows work required or recommended, and the sellers refuse to make all repairs, or a defect is too significant for buyers to go ahead with the purchase.
- The buyer and seller can't get together on price, closing date, or one of many other details of purchase issues.

- The sellers' or buyers' circumstances change significantly prior to closing.
- Lending issues or requirements fatally slow or halt the sale.
- Significant title or other property issues (special assessments, plans for new construction, and so on) exist or arise prior to closing.
- Buyers cannot sell their present home in time.

In a surprising number of these cases, those seeking to purchase ultimately find a new property and after closing (or even sooner) find that their new property is appreciably better for them.

Some of this is random luck. But often the better result on the second property is because the buyers have become better buyers, often much better buyers. They're better because of increased market knowledge, better because of increased knowledge of the real estate purchase transaction process. And often they're significantly better buyers because they are learning that emotions cloud judgment in real estate transactions and are best avoided.

Knowledge is power. And in real estate transactions, that translates into better deals and better finances.

We suggest using the gas tank rule. Knowledge gained from driving around a neighborhood, becoming familiar with the local real estate market and sale and listing prices, will ultimately save buyers at least $1,000 per tank of gas used. And that's for regular or low-fuel-efficiency vehicles. For hybrids and other high-efficiency vehicles, it's at least $2,000 savings per tank.

Something happens to those who listen and drive around. Knowledge grows. And grows. It can actually soar.

How many buyers are willing to expend ten or more tanks of gas and an equivalent amount of time looking at print ads and on the net searching for local real estate market information? Some. But we'll bet it's less than half of all buyers. For an informed buyer, a buyer who understands emotion and is able to control it, buying real estate is a highly productive process.

To be sure some properties are unique or very unusual. Buying your childhood home or that particular house you've always wanted to own can only happen when it goes on the market. Buying a place to vacation or live next door to other family members who already own property means your options are very limited. Some homes have remarkably attractive settings. Some homes have almost unique and highly appealing design or house layout features.

It's not surprising that emotion can drive purchase and price decision in those cases. For the large majority of other real estate decisions, full local market knowledge and fully controlled emotion produce the best results for buyers.

CHAPTER 13

Short Sales

RELATIVELY NEW ON THE foreclosure scene, short sales work this way.

A short-sale buyer—we'll call him Shorty—actively seeks to locate a borrower/owner who is underwater on a property (owes more than the property could sell for) and who ideally, from Shorty's perspective, is behind or struggling to make mortgage payments. After contacting the borrower/owner, Shorty submits a contingent offer (an offer with conditions) to buy the owner's property.

The principal conditions are these:

- Shorty will pay the owner $X for his property.
- The owner acknowledges that taking $X from Shorty is better than the looming or already started foreclosure and what it will do to him, his family, and his credit rating for a long time, possibly for life.
- The owner acknowledges he understands that the worst possible item on a credit report from a lender's perspective is a foreclosure and that it may preclude him from purchasing a home for at least seven years or at least from getting favorable financing.

- Shorty is obligated to do nothing unless the owner's lender(s) agrees in writing to accept $Y in full and complete satisfaction of all money owned by the owner to lender(s).
- Shorty is also obligated to do nothing if a large judgment, lien, or other large item affecting the title to the property appears before closing.
- The owner acknowledges that Shorty advised him to consult an attorney, particularly with regard to possible tax consequences of the offer to purchase, and any other advisor the owner would wish to consult with. Shorty refuses to let the owner accept Shorty's offer to purchase during the first seventy-two hours after it is presented.

Alternative to Foreclosure

On a property with a current value (what it would sell for today) of $250,000 and existing mortgages of $240,000, including accrued interest and late charges and delinquent taxes of $6,000, the owner, already unable to make all payments, is truly underwater. He probably knows there is no way he could receive as much as a dime if he tried to sell. In a sideways or declining real estate market, the mortgage balance figure could easily exceed current value, and the owner is that much more underwater.

In the above example, Shorty offers the owner $15,000 (which Shorty tactfully explains could be used for anything—living expenses, deposit on a new apartment, savings for a new home purchase someday, and so on), and offers the lender $135,000.

If Shorty's offer is accepted by owner *and* the lender, the transaction closes. Here is what happens.

The lender receives $135,000, clears its books, and gets regulators off its back. It avoids perhaps $20,000 in contested foreclosure legal fees, an additional year's taxes, an additional year's lost interest, a year's homeowner's insurance expense, property maintenance costs, possible weather damage, possible fire loss, possible vandalism loss and repair expenses, staff time and/or foreclosure management firm expenses, then expenses of sale of the foreclosed property into an uncertain real estate market.

The owner gets $15,000 to use for any purpose. All pending or approaching foreclosure proceedings are stopped or cut off at the pass, and any further credit damage is stopped. (Shorty's offer to the lender may even ask or require the lender to report owner's credit performance more favorably than would otherwise occur.) And the owner gets on with his life.

Shorty gets the property for $150,000 plus a $6,000 tax bill, which must be paid. Shorty knows of $10,000 in miscellaneous repair and maintenance work that will need to be done to bring the property up to saleable condition. He reckons it will take two months to sell the property for perhaps $220,000. He also knows there will be real estate commissions of perhaps 6 percent, as well as title insurance, taxes, and other expenses of sale totaling perhaps $6,000.

On these numbers, at the sale two months later in which the property goes for $220,000, Shorty gets a gross profit of $48,500, less costs of borrowing (if he used borrowed funds), other holding costs, and the expenses of sale which include real estate commission. Shorty knows he had time and expenses of locating the owner and the expenses of submitting seven other offers to other owners and lenders on other properties that were not accepted or fell apart, as well as legal fees. All this totaled $10,000.

Shorty figures he spends roughly twenty hours per month in his short-sale efforts and tries to meet or beat his goal of one closing every two and a half months.

Shorty will occasionally bump into one of his owners in a store or area fast-food restaurant and has yet to get a dirty look from any of them. He's usually too embarrassed to tell anyone about the tears and hugs from some of them.

You can see how short sales can make quite a change from what we previously thought was the usual foreclosure situation and result. They offer more options for owners, particularly if their short sale buyer is Shorty and not Shorty's tightwad cousin, who has a very high offers-to-purchase to closings ratio. The lender felt it at least had an option to consider in Shorty's offers. And the neighbors of the properties Shorty bought were (whether they knew it or not) certainly more fortunate than the neighbors of the properties with the long-drawn-out foreclosures.

Now let's turn back to the more usual circumstances in which you'll purchase foreclosed real estate.

CHAPTER 14

Before the Sale

BROADLY SPEAKING, there are three types of people who look to purchase foreclosures. The first group is made up of those who are seeking to buy a home to live in and are attracted to foreclosures because they are affordable. We call them *nesters*.

The second group includes people who already own a home but would change it if they could get a good buy in some area that represents upward mobility to them. We call people in this group *climbers*.

The third group is made up of individuals who want to buy for rental income and/or future appreciation. We would include in this group real estate professionals looking to buy low and sell high. In certain circles, this is called *flipping*. We call these people *pros*.

The Nesters

Many of the people in this group have almost no cash, little in the way of established credit, and employment records that are still developing. The need to have solid financing before venturing into an auction sale is unfortunately beyond many of these would-be auction buyers.

On the day of auction, a cashier's or certified check for at least 10 percent of the successful bid price is required; the balance is due within thirty days. That's a tall order for many.

Often, there is a belief that "a lender will loan the balance" after the 10 percent deposit is managed. This assumption ignores the fact that a property being sold at foreclosure auction has many problems the ordinary property does not have, including (but not limited to) difficulties with accessibility, ability to pass inspection, terminated utility services, possible hostile occupants, and general physical appearance.

Many people qualify as nesters. If the advice on bidding and auctions that follows in this chapter is unworkable for them, they should totally back away. They should set sights on the properties owned by lenders. It's sad to go the auction route only to learn that the commitment made will not be supported by any lender in your area. Some lenders will sometimes give generous terms on something they cannot unload in any other way if they think you can afford the property.

Nesters may not get the once-in-a-lifetime deal hoped for at foreclosure sale. But then again, realistic alternatives beat the unobtainable, and often lender-owned properties are better purchases. Going that route sure beats embarrassment and lost auction deposit money.

The Climbers

Likewise, those attempting to benefit from foreclosures in high-income areas are often unsuccessful. Foreclosures that take place in these neighborhoods are sometimes too expensive for the climbers—at foreclosure auction. Here too, the climber's best bet may be to wait out the foreclosure sale, or even attend it to see if the property ends up with the lender as the new owner. Then the climber can negotiate a purchase.

The Pros

Professionals (pros) are common attendees at foreclosure sales. These people, who do not have problems coming up with the funds to buy property, can be quite formidable competitors.

If you are a bidder at foreclosure auction, you could eventually find yourself in competition with members of this group. If they feel you are a novice, there is a chance that they will try to hurt you by bidding you up to pay a price that will prove to be a bad buy. They want to eliminate you as a future competitor.

The professionals in most places know each other and work within a loose network. This is not to say they are noncompetitive. Although they don't actually get together before sales to set limits, they still may have a general feel for whose "turn" it is to get the best of a deal.

You have to be pretty strong to buck them, but if you're prepared, you can protect yourself. (You can, for instance, pull out and leave an aggressive pro holding a bid that's too high. The pro will soon reconsider your status as a novice.)

Financing

Regardless of circumstances, if buyers are trying to secure a piece of property at foreclosure auction, they need to make arrangements before they bid so that they'll have the 10 percent bid money in cashier's or certified check and the balance in thirty days. Prearranged financing or ample liquid assets are absolutely the only way to go. The alternative is only for the very gutsy who don't mind losing big time. There are other words for gutsy, none of them complimentary in this context.

Consider a home equity loan on your present home; it may be one of the very best options open to you. If you own a home, you will learn—if you don't already know—that lenders are competing to loan money on what is basically a second mortgage on your present home. (Of course, if you have no existing mortgage, your financing options are even better.) Lenders will loan up to 80, 90, or even 100 percent of the appraised value less any existing mortgage, depending on your strength as a borrower.

You don't have to borrow the money immediately. You can go through the entire procedure, get a commitment for the total sum, and take out the cash only when you want to use it. The arrangement is similar to a business's line of credit at a bank. You can take money as needed and pay interest only each month on the unpaid balance. Monthly (interest only) payments are required only if there is an outstanding balance.

If you have reduced the principal balance outstanding and find a future need for funds, you can again borrow up to the original loan amount. Home equity loans can be drawn on or paid down frequently, even daily if the borrower wishes. The line-of-credit period is typically for five or ten years. At the end of that period, the loan will become a permanent loan, and you will then be required to retire it on a regular amortization basis (or consider getting a new line-of-credit loan).

In short, you can use any part of the money, when and if you need it. Let's say you use it to purchase and fix up property. You can then apply for a mortgage loan on the new property once you have made the most urgent of needed repairs and pay off the equity line-of-credit loan to use it again.

Or say you're a young single or couple seeking affordable housing. You may be able to get parents to make the home equity commitment and loan you the necessary funds for purchase. (Borrowed funds need to be disclosed as borrowed funds if a loan is being applied for to be part of the initial purchase price. The penalty provisions for a false application are very harsh.) When you're in title, you can apply for a permanent mortgage. There's one caution: If you're on title to a property already, a new loan on that property is actually a refinance.

On a conventional mortgage refinance, loan-to-value restrictions apply, and 100 percent financing is likely to be unavailable or pricey.

There are a couple of other avenues you can follow. The first is for parents to purchase the property as income or investment property in their own name. They can then contract to sell it to their child. As a purchaser, the child in this example may then qualify for as much as a 95 percent purchase mortgage loan.

A pending purchaser should consult a good local mortgage lender for permitted options for which they are qualified. In this example, when the child closes on the loan, the parents will receive the purchase price less their expenses of sale and cost of borrowing. Then all that's owed is heartfelt gratitude, and, in all likelihood, the parents will be overjoyed to have helped. Everyone will be happy, and the child will have encountered one of life's win-win situations.

"Hard-Money" Lenders

Of course, only some are in a position to take advantage of such an arrangement. Let's talk now about hard-money lenders, also known as *factors*. The greater the risk, the greater the lender's return must be. There are local lenders who can be contacted ahead of time to give the needed loan commitment to lend on a foreclosure sale purchase. But remember that this is not an easy situation. You should have highly trusted referrals before you consider going this route.

Let's assume you are the pending purchaser/borrower in this situation. You haven't bid yet. There's no certainty that yours will be the winning bid, and there's no guarantee what that bid amount will be.

These are not insurmountable problems, but you may have to spend some money on inspections, despite the fact that the property may never be yours. Other than that, the question boils down to cost and risk. You give the lender your financial information in advance; if all checks out, you learn how much you may borrow.

Any commitment that is given is based on your credit (although the lender may not make all the money available to you if the property is somehow questionable). The money the lender advances is not long term, and it's at a higher rate than the customary mortgage. Loan fees are often more, too. Before you get angry, stop and think.

The lender is making it possible for you to buy a property at foreclosure auction. The rate will be appreciably higher than that charged by other lenders—but the other lenders won't take this kind of risk!

The reason for the short length of the mortgage is that you're expected to go out for a permanent loan once you've acquired title and made the improvements. So don't be horrified; say, "Thank you"! At least your interest payments lessen when you pay off the hard-money loan.

In business, manufacturers borrow from hard-money lenders on a continuous basis and are happy to get the loans. They help the companies stay in business, and the borrowers know it. Hard-money lenders, if used properly, can make some pretty impossible-sounding dreams come true. Remember the need for highly trusted referrals if you are considering going this route.

Lawyers and the Auction Sale

People often ask whether they should take a lawyer with them to an auction sale. The answer is probably no. There's not much an attorney will be able to do for you at the actual foreclosure sale. An attorney may well suggest her presence isn't necessary at foreclosure sales, particularly once you become familiar with the ropes. You need to use your attorney long before you get to the foreclosure sale. Foreclosure sale terms are published; they won't be altered. We believe in using lawyers—in fact, we consider attorneys an absolute necessity—and do so in all real estate transactions. Much of their value to you will be in counseling and education and having you run transactions and documents past them before you sign. An attorney can also add value by being available for cell phone questions as needed rather than actual physical presence at each meeting or auction.

An explanation of a title insurance policy is in order here. The policy that insures your ownership of real estate is called by different names, depending on what part of the country you're in. *Title insurance policy* and *fee policy* are the most common.

If you get a mortgage from a lender at the time you purchase the property, or get a refinance loan, you will also pay for a title insurance policy for the lender. That title insurance policy called a lender's policy insures that you own the property and also insures the lender's mortgage. It insures only the lender, and provides no insurance coverage to you, the buyer. Over and above that required insurance, you should agree to pay for a title insurance policy that insures you. This policy is called an owner's title insurance policy, and it is the one that insures you, the owner.

We know of no reason to not pay for and have the protection of an owner's title insurance policy.

In essence, you are insuring that you actually own (have good title to) the property you have purchased. If any person or organization materializes with a valid claim to the property that overrides yours, the title company makes good. Such coverage is an absolute necessity in a foreclosure purchase. The title insurance company makes certain that you are informed of claims against title to a particular property before you put your money and credit on the line so you can make the correct decisions early, not after it's too late. Check with your local title insurance company to get information on the varieties of coverage available. We recommend you use the title insurance company that your attorney uses. Your attorney and the title insurance company will protect your interests, but only if you have them and use them in forming your decisions and do this before you act.

Inspector's Reports

These days in a standard (nonforeclosure) purchase of a property, before you are obligated to close on the purchase, you'll be advised to get an inspector's report. Inspections now are a matter of course in almost all regular real estate sales and are highly useful if you can get them before you bid at a foreclosure sale as well as in any pre- or post-foreclosure you are considering.

But access problems often mean they are simply unavailable before an actual foreclosure sale. In the early years of our real estate business, no one had ever heard of an inspector's report. People looked houses over and bought them. We didn't hear anyone complain of buying a "pig in a poke."

Now you'll be advised to get a report even before you bid on the property at a foreclosure auction. This means that if you don't win with your bid, or if you run into some snag that has nothing to do with the report (and these are not uncommon developments), you will have paid to inspect a property you will never own. Moreover, the defaulting borrowers or other tenants may be in possession of the building and may refuse to let any inspector enter.

If you want to have an inspector check the house after you've bought it, by all means do so. But to be contrary for a moment, ask yourself what the inspection is going to tell you after you already own the property. That the plumbing leaks? That the furnace is shot? That the electrical system needs to be upgraded?

Are these things you wouldn't deduce on your own? You've just purchased a foreclosed house. You know it may need some work.

That inspection fee will pay a portion of the plumber's bill. And the furnace company will check your heating system and tell you what repairs are needed; after it's fixed, the repairman will usually offer you a service contract. There are a lot of good electricians out there who can check the wiring and do what's necessary for you. They may not be able to turn out a fancy report, though.

All this being said, we've seen more than a handful of instances in which an inspector's report saved a regular purchaser with an accepted offer to purchase a property from big time headaches, such as a bowed roof, significant basement flaws, or other major repairs needed.

For pre- or post-foreclosure sales from lenders, an inspection report is often of great value. We recommend going one better and having your contractor or handyperson who will be doing the actual work inspect for you as well. The nature of foreclosure sales means inspection reports will often be unavailable to you when the moment comes for you to bid or be silent.

Inspecting Vacant Properties

It is not uncommon for the property being foreclosed to be vacant. The mortgagors abandon the property; perhaps a neighbor notifies the lender or the foreclosing attorney out of concern that vandals may torch the property and put other homes in danger.

The lender sends a crew out to board up the house and secure it, although it does not own the property at this point. It is merely taking steps to protect an investment. No one wants to see the home become the target of neighborhood kids or a domicile for transients.

It may actually be possible to contact the lender and arrange for an inspection of the property if it is vacant. Obviously, there are significant risks in taking on an abandoned house. In this case, with lender-permitted access, you should definitely inspect the property yourself before you make any commitment. If you are determined to buy the place and cannot inspect, at least interview the neighbors. They might have been inside and may have some sense about the place.

At a promotional event in New York City, we met a very bright woman who told of recently buying a foreclosure in a very high-rent area. We asked, "Were you able to inspect it?" She said no, that she had gone on a gut feeling and bought it at the sheriff's sale for $150,000. After less than $75,000 in repairs and upgrades, she said it is now worth nearly $1 million, even in the current challenging market. That is gutsy buying. And a great result. But it's risky.

One largely overlooked matter is environmental and zoning problems. Such difficulties are showing up with greater and greater frequency and may very well be the reason a borrower walked away from a property.

You're probably already familiar with the horror stories about radon, asbestos removal, gasoline contamination from nearby storage tanks, underground storage tanks on site, and the like. Do a little creative research; make sure you're not walking into a nightmare.

Some years ago, a fellow offered one of us a very attractive property at what seemed like a remarkably low price. Some research showed that the deal that seemed to be too good to be true really was. A trip to the state department of transportation yielded the information that a proposed roadway was slated to pass right through the house. The offer was declined. It's not fun or cheap negotiating a good condemnation price from the department of transportation

The possibility exists that the property you have your eye on breaches local zoning laws. These violations will have to be corrected before you complete a sale of the property, and they might be costly. Don't wait for the title company to tell you that the two-family house you bought is zoned as a one-family house. You may already have the winning bid at the foreclosure sale. Take a trip to the town's building department and confirm that you are looking at a legal two-family unit. Do this before the sale.

It may be possible that you are looking at a two-family house in an area that is zoned one family. You may have a situation here that precedes the date of the zoning laws and is permitted because certificates of occupancy for two-family houses weren't issued at that time.

In this case, if you are planning to use the income from both units in your application for your long-term financing, it's possible that the lender will not count the rental income. In the event of major fire or wind damage to the property, the town may not permit you to restore it as a two-family property. The new construction must conform to the present zoning restrictions. When you buy this type of property, you are taking that risk. Time spent at city hall can save some expensive mistakes.

Junior Liens

Other parties may have a security interest in the property being foreclosed; be prepared to encounter junior liens on the property. You can often expect a second mortgage holder to bid the price up to a level that will protect their interest, even if they have to buy the property themselves for more than they are owed if the local real estate market is very strong.

It's also likely they won't want to buy the property—they'll simply want the money owed and hope that the auction price will be high enough so they at least get some money if someone else buys the property.

Don't let the fact that there is a second mortgage keep you away from a property you want. There's no guarantee that second lien holders will be at the sale. Occasionally they will have been paid off. Or the second mortgage holder may simply decide not to bid at all. There is only one way to be absolutely certain: Attend the sale. Just remember, you need to know exactly what you will be getting if you bid at a foreclosure sale. More than one buyer has been sadly surprised and wished he had consulted a title company and attorney before bidding.

CHAPTER 15

Preparing for the Sale

NOW THAT YOU HAVE done the improvements and upgrades, it is time to sell—unless you bought the property as an owner occupant or are holding it to rent. Most folks will not keep the properties they acquire because they knew from the beginning that they would not hold them as rental properties or for sale into a later/better market. (Holding for sale into a better market is the right idea only for highly attractive properties in terrific locations.) So let's assume it is sell time for your property.

So, how are you going to do it? Will you do it on your own, as a "for sale by owner" (FSBO) deal? Will you use a limited-service broker, or will you use a full-service real estate broker? Here are your options.

For Sale By Owner (FSBO)

The owner puts out a sign and places ads in the local newspaper. There is no commission involved because there is no real estate agent involved. And there is no multiple listing service (MLS) exposure. MLS is the information system owned by a local group of real estate brokers to make that property available for sale by every member broker and sales associate in its membership, according to MLS rules, including sharing or splitting of commissions. If the property is entered in MLS, every member broker and their sales associate in the area has the chance to sell a property and be compensated for doing that.

But with the FSBO option, that exposure is not there. FSBO is for those who will not pay for anything other than the most limited market exposure. Some FSBOs sell, but it generally takes many more days on the market, and it is highly unlikely that very restricted market exposure will produce a satisfying price. The property owner is responsible for all marketing, selling, and negotiating, as well as lending, appraising, and inspection issues, contract forms, drafting, and all aspects of closing. Most FSBO sellers have sold fewer than three properties in their lives.

Limited Service Brokerage

There are many types of limited brokerage available, all at a discounted commission. All put property into MLS for an up-front fee and charge the balance of their total fees at closing. The seller usually does all the advertising, showing, negotiating, and selling except proofing the offer to purchase, which is done by the broker. This system relies on the MLS system exposure to produce a buyer for the property. The seller pays a commission, which is higher if another MLS broker finds the buyer, but is less than if a full service brokerage is used.

Full Service Brokerage

Almost all the high-profile real estate companies are full-service brokers. Full service means those firms do everything to produce a sale. The seller only has to approve the offers to purchase presented and sign documents at closing. Commissions are typically 6 to 7 percent of the final sales price.

The listing company lists at whatever commission schedule it charges, and the selling company, usually called a co-broke or selling broker, gets a split of that commission, usually between 2.4 and 3 percent of the final sales price.

So, if the listing company offers 2.4 percent to any selling company, what does the listing company keep? It retains the difference between the 2.4 percent and the listing broker's commission, say 6 percent. Sometimes, but not generally, the broker's commission can be a specified dollar amount.

But what about the listing limited-service broker compensation? Remember they are getting some money up front. They also generally charge the seller 2.4 percent of the sales price and pay it to the selling company if the property is sold by a selling broker and not the listing broker. So in a limited-service broker contract, the total commission depends on the following factors: who sells the property, and the total compensation agreed to at the time the limited-service listing was signed.

There are other things you must know when you sell. A seller will be paying for a title insurance policy, the part of this year's real estate taxes through the date of closing, a real estate transfer tax or deed stamps, and maybe other charges as well. Each of these fees varies with state and locality.

How does a seller or buyer go about choosing a real estate agent? There is no shortcut to making a good choice. It takes the same time, effort, and willingness to make inquiries that choosing any other professional does. There are two types of agency contracts in the real estate business. An agent is by contract an agent of either the seller or the buyer. Most agents are agents of the seller and are paid commission by the seller. In other words, the agent's responsibility is to get the best price and to represent the seller's interests, and the seller only, not the buyer. Remember this. The other type is agency for the buyer, or buyer's agency. Remember, an agent's responsibility is to represent his/her principal's interests. It is the same as appointing an attorney. Just as an attorney becomes a specific person's lawyer, a real estate agent becomes either a seller's or a buyer's agent.

Sign a buyer-agency contract if such a contract is in fairly widespread use in your area. It is often not to a buyer's advantage to use a buyer agent broker if use of a buyer agency is rare in your area. And stay with the agent and your contract! Remember, once you sign that contract, you have appointed that agent to find you a property.

A party signing a buyer-agency contract may be obligated to pay that agent a commission even if the buyer himself finds a property on a Sunday morning drive. It is the same thing for a seller with a listing contract if the selling owner finds a buyer in a bar on a Saturday night unless the listing contract says otherwise. And remember, a seller should list with one agent only, not two.

If you have signed a buyer-agency contract, you have committed to pay that agent a commission upon a successful purchase closing. But remember you are obligated to the contract you have signed. We have seen too many buyers violate that agreement and run around with other agents, or go on their own, even though they may be under a contract.

If you are buying, you either sign a buyer-agency contract with an agent who represents you in all negotiations, or you do not sign a buyer-agency contract. Then every agent you encounter will be an agent of the seller. Either relationship can work for you, but the differences are enormous. You must understand your relationship with agents to have this work to your advantage. Remember this.

Agents have access to the MLS and also know values. We think it important that you have an agent, a title company, and an attorney on your team. (See Appendix C for an example of a buyer-agency contract.)

So, here is what you must decide: Do I want to pay a commission even though I located and bought the property on my own? Since most people are trying to eliminate a commission, it is critical that you specify in the contract that you will pay the commission to that buyer's agent only if he procured the property. That leaves you on the search and leaves the agent on the search. If your agent locates the place, of course, he has earned the commission. However, if you do not specify the conditions, you owe the commission no matter who found the place. As Professor Harold Hill stated, "You gotta know the territory"—the territory in this case being the buyer-agency contract.

Now, here are two more critical things to know.

Agent Relationships

Those reading this book who have experience selling real estate know that a high percentage of buyers do not want to work inside a buyer-agency contract, but they want agents to locate a home for them. The reality is that most buyers are running around with more than one agent, going through open houses, calling owners—in other words, searching on their own. Many people use the agent for information, but they have no concern whether that agent is ever paid. We in the business are alert to that conduct and can generally spot it early on. Many agents will not work with a buyer unless he or she enters into a buyer-agency contract. We are explaining this so you know how to create an agent relationship that will benefit you.

When you meet an agent you feel is the one you want, explain how you want to work with that agent. Detail exactly what you want that agent to do for you and what you will do in return. Do you want an exclusive search, meaning you, the buyer, owe the agent a commission no matter who locates the property you purchase? If you want a limited search, meaning that you as the buyer will search also, you must specify and agree that you will pay only if the agent locates the sale property. See what is mutually agreeable.

Next, if you want fully committed service to you, explain that you want that agent to sell your property when the time comes, and assure the agent that you will abide by your word. You want the agent to work for you.

CHAPTER 16

The Sale

FORECLOSURE SALES CAN be held just about anywhere that is centrally located and accessible. They are typically held on the courthouse steps (weather permitting). By the way, when a notice refers to the courthouse steps, it really does mean the steps outside the building. If you're in any doubt as to whether the front or rear steps are being used, ask a receptionist or guard for directions.

Be early. It is often far too late to arrive at 9:03 for a sale that is scheduled for 9 A.M. Don't take the chance that the parade will pass you by. Show up well before the appointed time. (The day before the sale is scheduled, you should call the office of the foreclosing attorney to confirm that the sale is still on.)

Chances are that you won't be alone on the steps. You've thought the property worthy of consideration, and you can expect others to do the same. The sale will begin with a recital of the terms of sale. After this brief description of the terms of sale is concluded, the sale begins. It may be over in as little as three minutes. You can see now why promptness is so essential.

Buying from the Winning Bidder

We discussed the pros a little earlier, those regulars who purchase properties, fix them up, and then offer them for sale. We can tell you something about these bidders: They know their markets. What's more, they know what to expect once they've purchased the property. They know how to cope with problems.

They are not buying the property to live in, however. That may be a very important piece of information for you.

If yours is not the winning bid (or if you choose not to bid at all because of cash constraints), you can speak to the winner at the sale site and make a commitment to buy it from the winner, then and there, subject to an inspection that shows no major repairs needed or vandalism damage. You'll be saving the pro money. All the pro is putting out at that time is the 10 percent down payment. He'll have a very short holding period while you're getting the inspection and finalizing your financing, and he may pass some of the savings on to you. Under these circumstances, you can often make a highly favorable purchase. The winning bidder is often happy to give you some time to secure permanent financing—and you may be able to get valuable information from this person on the best sources for that mortgage money, as well.

The reason we're suggesting that you speak to these people is that they usually offer their properties at a far more competitive price than the rest of the market. They know what is moving and for how much; they tend to price their properties below that level to assure a quick sale. What's more, they are eager to find buyers quickly; holding properties for a long time dissipates profit potential. Unlike homeowners who are emotionally tied to the homes they've lived in, these operators do not fall in love with the merchandise. They are engaged in a business venture. If you can help them turn a quick profit, they'll be amenable to your purchase offer.

Don't latch on to the first professional you meet; make the effort to get to know a few of them. Some of these folks are knowledgeable, reasonable businesspeople; others would tear the wings off butterflies for relaxation. Let the buyer beware. Reduce all agreements to writing, no matter how charming your contact is. Show everything to your attorney before signing.

The Bidding

The opening bid price at the auction is called the *upset price.* This price is generally determined by the amount due the lender, which would include the mortgage balance, all charges for late payments, plus costs incurred in the foreclosure action such as legal fees, title charges, process service, publication, and other expenses. Add it all together and you have the amount that is due the lender. At the sale, a representative of the lender usually opens the bid. This person makes the opening bid in the event no one else does. That bid of the lender will be the upset price.

A representative of the lender *usually* opens the bid. Occasionally, though, a mortgagee will not bid in at the sale. It hardly seems logical that someone who is owed money secured by real property would refuse to bid on the property. What underlies such a strategy? The answer lies in the fact that, as a creditor, the mortgagee is not charged with the responsibilities of ownership.

If the lender knows there are building or health-code violations or derelict automobiles strewn about the front yard that must be disposed of or property damage for example, it may not bid on the property in question. As long as the lender is not in title, it's just another aggrieved party. Once the lender becomes the owner, it has all the responsibilities of ownership.

If there are no advantages, from the lender's point of view, in owning, there may be no lender bid, and, assuming no one else wants the property, it may end up with the taxing authorities.

The lesson for you? If you do not hear a bid from the lender to start things off, beware. They may know something you don't. Some properties are more of a liability than an asset. Don't let the thrill of buying at a low price make the decision for you.

Postponements

Last-minute postponement of foreclosure sales is not uncommon. Often, the foreclosure sale will be resolved or postponed at the eleventh hour, and the lender or attorney or other party may or may not appear on the steps to express apologies to those who showed up for the sale. Of course, these plans can be changed again. If you're interested in the property, keep in touch with the attorney or receiver. Sometimes the only thing holding up the sale is a legal technicality that must be attended to.

Who Gets the Auction Sale Money?

As we have seen, lenders are not out to foreclose property to make a profit at the foreclosure sale. The lender can only receive the amount it is owed at an auction sale. That is usually the amount of the upset price; the overage at a foreclosure sale is known as *surplus money.*

Surplus money is paid out to the junior lien holders in the order of the priority of their liens and then to the previous owner if there is any left over. A junior lien holder who knows that the property was sold for a price in excess of the amount owed the first mortgage holder can't simply sit back and wait for a check; there is a process known as a surplus money proceeding, in which the junior lien holder makes an application through the court for its claim. It's the obligation of the junior lien holder to make claim and certify that the debt in question was never repaid.

Other Costs

What other costs will the buyer at auction have? Well, virtually none, if you want to live like a Mississippi riverboat gambler. There are some outlays you should make, however, to protect yourself, and chief among these is a title insurance policy. Title insurance is your protection against someone's challenging your right to ownership of the property.

If you've managed to find a lender to fund your purchase, that lender will require a title insurance policy, but this will not protect you. It will only protect the lending institution. Protect yourself as well, with an owner's title insurance policy.

Suppose you've paid someone to do a title search and it's come up clean; there is no record of any snag in the chain of ownership of the property. The coast appears to be clear. No one seems to have any grounds to challenge your title. Why should you pay extra for title insurance when you're already in possession of all the facts and have found nothing to worry about?

There's only one reason, but it's a compelling one that overrides everything. You pay to protect yourself against what hasn't shown up in the record and could come forth and be a valid, sustainable objection to title or at least turn out to be one heck of an expensive nuisance. It is true that these claims are quite rare. Some of the reasons that have surfaced have been so farfetched as to seem inconceivable. But it could happen to you, and even an illegitimate claim has to be defended. That costs money and time and may prevent you from selling. If you don't have title insurance, you'll have to pay any claim or expenses of defending any challenge out of your own pocket. If you do get the insurance, however, the title company will send its lawyers to represent you no matter what the claim is, just as in an auto accident case. If the claim is held to be valid, the company will pay what it takes to preserve your title, up to the amount of the title insurance policy, which typically is the total price you paid for the property.

No one will require you to buy title insurance. (If you have a lender, it will require that you pay for a lender's title insurance policy.) But if you don't want to purchase an owner's title insurance policy, we recommend that you don't buy real estate. Too many titles have been clouded by missing heirs, creditors, forged documents, and who knows what else to take the risk.

Usually, the only other charge you'll need to consider as a foreclosure sale buyer is that of recording your deed. Again, this is not required unless you have a lender. But if you fail to record the deed, the public has no notice that the property has been transferred. You've just purchased a property that had a previous owner who was in all kinds of financial hot water. If you don't record your deed and put an end to that ownership as far as the public record is concerned, you may find that a few more unwelcome claims against the property have materialized. This is not the time to pinch pennies. Your best course is to record the deed immediately. (Note: If you choose to buy title insurance, you don't have the option of not paying to record the deed; the title company will see that this happens.)

A little more background is probably in order about title insurance. In a foreclosure judgment, the court appoints or statute designates a party to conduct the sale. By statute this party has the power to sell the property and to sign a valid, legally acceptable deed (known as a *referee's deed, sheriffs deed,* or a similar name). When the authorized party signs that deed, any interest of the previous owner is terminated. The new owner has title, but there's more.

Most deeds contain covenants, warranties, and agreements that are passed along with the deed by the previous owner. A sheriff's deed by whatever name doesn't contain any such covenants and warranties; it conveys title, period. The title insurance company is not providing any title insurance protection as to zoning or occupancy matters. They take on insuring you have marketable title, not your right to occupy the property as it exists.

The title insurance company is insuring (and agrees to defend at its expense) your legal title to the property, and nothing more. You can't even look to the lender for redress as to, for example, a zoning violation because you didn't really buy the property from the lender. (In fact, you were in competition with it.)

There is always the potential for zoning or building code violations. These are excepted by the title company. *Excepted* means that the company is not insuring as to these items, and you cannot look to the title insurance company for correction of those problems.

When the title insurance company in writing (usually in its preliminary report of title, which is called a title commitment or written commitment to issue a final policy subject to recording final documents and other conditions it specifies) tells you that it is excepting something, make sure you understand what this means to you. Ask questions.

Exceptions on your title policy don't mean that you won't get marketable title. They are simply the title company's way of eliminating their responsibility for problems that may arise with regard to the items specified. Run these items past your attorney before you proceed.

Congratulations!

The title got your attorney's blessing. Your financing worked without a hitch and you are now the proud owner of a foreclosed property. What's next?

CHAPTER 17

After the Sale

IF YOU ROLLED THE DICE and acquired a property at a good price, one you hope is low enough to offset the risks of acquiring without access and an inspection, you now have other issues to handle. There may be holdover occupancy by the previous owners or possibly by tenants. These tenants may have a lease not terminated by the foreclosure depending on the language in the lease. In a few locations throughout the country, there also could be rent control issues. Holdover owners could have their lives torn apart by foreclosure and other financial and emotional distress. Because state practice varies, we are not going to advise you on the ins and outs of getting people out of the property in your locale.

In any of these circumstances, you need legal advice. Do yourself a favor and get a lawyer who knows the eviction process. Find someone with plenty of experience in landlord/tenant matters. Remember that even a lawyer who specializes in real estate may not know the proper procedure for removing unwanted holdover owners or tenants without a legal right to remain in the property.

How do you find the best lawyer for the job? Ask around. Ask the clerk of courts for leads. Such attorneys appear before the court on a regular basis. In most locales a relatively small number of attorneys handle a high percentage of landlord/tenant occupancy matters. The lawyer you are likely to end up with through this route is probably not going to give you any problems when it comes to spending the required amount of time in court. There are probably six other cases the attorney needs to try at the same time.

Don't ask your college roommate attorney to handle the job for you. You probably will regret such a choice and probably spend far too much money. You won't give offense; your old college roommate probably is not a specialist in this area and would rather focus on other parts of his or her practice, anyway.

Remember, it's always easier to get into real estate than to get out. A great price on a so-so property is a terrible deal. Buying a property as your own home? It's best to buy only if the property makes your heart sing. Buying for rental or quick sale? Don't do it unless you at least hear music.

Surprise, Surprise

People often resent moving out of a foreclosed property. Sometimes they express their resentment in strange and very damaging ways. We can't begin to tell you some of the things former owners have done to properties. If we did, this book would probably be X-rated. Let's just say that former owners can perform outrageous acts of vandalism. There is at least one way to possibly mitigate vandalism, at least after you acquire title. One of the necessary simultaneous acts of home ownership is securing an insurance policy. The moment you take title, you own the property; you must have prearranged insurance coverage in effect.

Do not close your acquisition transaction until you have insurance coverage in place. You can get extended coverage on your policy to cover vandalism and malicious mischief, which, it should be noted, can happen even if the prior owners moved out without incident. You may have to show the property to someone else: a lender, a contractor, or an appraiser, for instance. You do not want to conduct a tour for others of a vandalized property, so be sure to look things over beforehand. Make whatever repairs are necessary or at least alert your visitors that they will be seeing a mess. If you can't do cleanup and repairs yourself, consider getting a legitimate estimate from a contractor.

Wells and Septic Systems

What if you are considering a property with a well and septic system? How should you proceed? What if you cannot inspect prior to purchase; will you roll the dice? Here is an example of what can occur. We once sold a property with well and septic. The seller provided a safe water test. The buyers did have access to inspect, so they got a professional septic inspection, which disclosed no defects.

A week after the buyers acquired the property and moved in, the septic system backed up. After hiring another inspector, the buyer learned that the septic system on this property was a failed system. How could that happen?

Here is how. Some inspectors will simply look down the stack for standing water. If they see no standing water, to them it means the percolation is successful, and it is a functional system. If they see standing water, it means percolation is a failure and the system is therefore a failed system. This first inspection showed no standing water and passed. The previous owner knew how to make the system pass. He knew how the inspection procedure worked, so he simply stopped using the dishwasher and the washing machine. He worked out and showered at a local athletic club.

Gather Information

Real clinkers like this are less than a 10 percent risk, but you must still use all your info-gathering skills. Then ask two friends to do a drive-by of the property and area. Ask them to be completely candid. After they have done their drive-bys, ask them to point their thumbs down, up, or horizontal. If the score is less than one up and one horizontal forget it. If there is one horizontal thumb, ask him or her to tilt slightly up or down depending on how they feel about the property. If there is hesitation or a tilt even slightly down, don't buy the place.

Again, we strongly recommend acquiring property only with purchase price and working capital funds prearranged. You will need to include cost of repairs and holding expenses until occupancy and sale of a previous residence, if you have one.

Do the math carefully. It's how you and your family will be living while financially vulnerable. Go into battle only with your powder dry—your financing prearranged.

You may have financed your new property with a line of credit instead of a home equity loan, and in this case only a local bank, savings bank, or credit union active in real estate lending is likely to meet your needs. Your lender will take a mortgage on the new property and also a simultaneous second mortgage on your present residence or other assets you own. Those without a solid equity position, solid verifiable income, good credit standing, other financial assets (savings or retirement funds), and other debt obligations under control need not apply. The lender and/or you will be providing 100 percent of the purchase price, plus additional working and holding expenses. If the lender can't see the math work, you won't be approved. Nor should you want to try and go into an untenable position.

Assuming you are buying a property to occupy as your residence, soon after getting title with your line of credit or home equity loan, you will be anxious to acquire long-term financing on the new property. But let's assume the sale of your old residence still hasn't occurred. This experience will remind you why it is important to have prearranged financing. This is serious stuff; you don't want to expose yourself, your spouse, or your family to hardship.

Sale of your old residence requires a combination of factors:

- Excellent current knowledge of your local real estate market for comparable properties
- Realistic pricing
- A dedicated real estate agent with this knowledge
- Blind luck
- A real estate market so hot virtually anything sells instantly, in which case you may sell for too little

Again, we feel it makes no sense to sell an expensive asset without an appraisal. Let's say you inherited a Ferrari with some racing history and you know you want to sell it. Or you inherited an original painting by an artist with a national reputation. Or you inherited stock in a corporation whose shares don't trade publicly.

Does it make sense not to have a good appraisal or appraisals?

Now, let's sell your house. It's a five-, six-, or seven-figure real estate asset, perhaps your most valuable possession. There are only four conditions under which you should even consider selling without an appraisal:

1. You work your area and track and know all real estate activity in your area of similar properties, information usually only available from Multiple Listing Services. Alternately, you are highly personable and can talk people into sharing honest sales price info that some folks consider confidential and will not want to disclose.

2. Your home is virtually identical to nearby homes that sold recently, and homeowner improvements are also similar.
3. You have a firm and accurate sense of whether the market in your area is accelerating, slowing, or holding steady.
4. Your best friend is a well-regarded professional appraiser in your town, the least biased person you have ever met, and has gratuitously provided you with a long-form appraisal with four or more comparable properties identical to yours that sold recently within 900 yards or less of your property.

We cannot overemphasize the importance of having an appraisal prior to sale (contrasted with an appraisal ordered by a buyer or lender to support a sales transaction where the price has already been agreed to).

Even with such an appraisal, properties will often sell for more or less than the appraised value. At least you and others who go this route will have the best possible pricing guidance available. You can get far less useful information from a bunch of sources, including words heard over the fence or at a neighborhood cocktail party. If that mode of gathering information is the basis for your major financial decision, best of luck to you.

Astoundingly, the large majority of properties sold in this country are sold without benefit of an advance appraisal. The huge majority of appraisals are done after sale and are required by lenders to support the loan. If your purpose for buying property is to sell for profit (after the property has been brought up to sale condition), or you are selling your present home, the choice of method of sale is yours:

- List your property for sale with a full-service Realtor specializing in homes in your projected sales price range in your area.
- List with a limited-service broker, knowing the limited service will require you or others on your behalf to perform almost all the sales and negotiation functions.

- Pop up your own for sale sign with your phone number and hope limited market exposure will still result in a sales price you consider acceptable, knowing that you or others on your behalf will perform all sales and other functions including supervising the closing.

There are advantages to each approach.

Option one includes full market exposure and performance of all sales functions.

Option two also provides Multiple Listing Service exposure and performance of some other limited specified functions.

Option three means that all proceeds of the sale are yours.

The percentage of final sales price you retain is, of course, dependent on the sales method you select. Selling the property on your own, if you're successful, leaves you with 100 percent of the net proceeds of the sales price. Discount brokerage, if successful, results in a sale that is probably triggered by the Multiple Listing Service exposure, with sales price again primarily your doing. And full-service brokerage, if successful, has your selected agent as your negotiating agent acting on your behalf through the entire process, including negotiations leading to sale, appraisal, inspection, and loan matters. It also includes negotiations over repairs or replacements, changes in closing dates, title issues, if any, and closing mechanics.

Which route is the best way to go? Here's a realistic way to decide. Assume someone else, someone near and dear to you, owns the property. Would you recommend to that person that you try to sell that person's property using method three?

Would you recommend that you try to sell it for that person using method two?

Would you recommend that person obtain the services of the best full-service agent and firm in your area?

If you feel comfortable enough in your knowledge of property values, your sales and negotiating skills, and your knowledge of transaction and closing mechanics, then consider selecting method three or method two.

If answering the above questions makes you doubt your capability to effectively represent that person, why would you recommend yourself as the seller of their property?

Let's be very honest here. If you are, selecting the best choice for the sale of your property is really quite easy. And you will make the correct decision. We're sure of it.

You've probably guessed we consider sales methods two and three to be very risky unless you have a lot of general real estate knowledge including current sales prices in your area. You must know your numbers. You must know what a place is worth when you buy. You must know what it will be worth if you decide to sell, and you must have a good handle on the expenses and holding costs in between.

CHAPTER 18

Calculating a Bid Price for Investment Property

IN DETERMINING WHAT you want to bid for a property, you must take into consideration the use to which it will be put. A buyer intending to live in the property can be expected to pay more than someone seeking to use it for investment purposes. This chapter examines the investment-type bid.

You may intend to turn the property over for a profit, and quickly. We recommend that you plan on using real estate brokers to help you sell; you can use all the market exposure you can get. Include the broker's commission in your calculations. Only brokers affiliated with the Multiple Listing Service provide broad market exposure.

Allow time in your calculations. Even under the most favorable conditions, time has a habit of slipping away. Unforeseen delays are costly, yet they occur, and you must provide for them.

If you're going to do work on the property or have that work done for you, make sure that you establish deadlines. Make it absolutely clear that terms of payment depend on the contractor's ability to adhere to those completion dates. Contractors have a habit of starting several jobs at once and delaying all of them while they seek new business.

Never make the mistake of giving a large advance deposit to a contractor. If the contractor runs a small business and tells you that funds are needed to buy materials, have him select the materials. Have them shipped directly to you, and pay the supplier. At least you have the materials if the project drags on indefinitely.

Remember: While the property is unoccupied, you are paying for taxes and for insurance. Figure these elements into your calculations. Smart sellers usually use six months as a time frame in a balanced market. And of course you need to know your local market and its direction. If there's a lot to be done, you might do well to extend the time frame to nine months, again in a balanced market.

Start at the top. How much do you think the property would be worth if you brought it to tip-top condition? Can you price it below the market so it moves more quickly than any other comparable property that's up for sale? If not, you should ask yourself another question: Why are you even thinking of purchasing?

Repairs that Add the Most Value

For a property that you're intending to resell, it's a good idea to pay particularly close attention to the kitchens and bathrooms. These are the areas of the house that draw the greatest interest from prospective buyers. Beyond that, if you can carpet the floors, do so. Get a neutral color carpet that will blend with many decors.

With a property that needs sprucing up, don't make the mistake of putting off painting because "people will want to choose their own colors." Your objective is to avoid negative perceptions and comments from potential buyers. Believe us, you'll get back every dollar of your expenditure in higher selling price and reduced waiting time.

Other Cost Concerns

With respect to the costs of sale through your real estate agent, each locality has its own standards. Commissions may be set by agreement within a market area. Your commission will depend on what you agree to. You should know the commission needed to attract aggressive selling attention.

Legal charges are established by agreement with your attorney. (A good real estate agent can also be depended on to recommend attorneys you are likely to be pleased with.) Select the professionals (contractors, real estate brokers, attorneys, accountants, and so on) who will work with you based solely on price if that method has always worked for you before and you have retained a lot of professionals.

Stamps on deeds or transfer taxes are either state or local revenue charges. Practices differ from area to area. Do your homework so you will be prepared for these and other customary charges, including title insurance and recording fees.

Holding costs are an area in which many prospective investors get hurt. Be sure you provide for taxes, insurance, and interest, utilities, and other items during the holding period.

Take the checklists at the end of this book with you when you examine a property. See if you can estimate what is needed; allow yourself a reasonable figure to accomplish whatever must be done. Estimate high, and then give yourself an additional 22 percent cushion.

Even if you're going to do some of the work yourself, estimate what a professional would charge and use that figure. You might plan initially to take care of certain items only to find that you don't have the time, inclination, or skill. Give yourself a cushion; budget as though you're planning on using a professional. Talk to plumbers, painters, installers, and other service providers and get a ballpark estimate to work with. Armed with all this information, you'll be able to set the upper limit of your bid.

The "Overall Cost of Purchase" checklist provided in Appendix B should help you collect all the information you need to know to make an informed decision. (Of course, if you find that there isn't room for adequate profit, you should not make the bid at all!) And make sure your projected profit figure is the one we recommend.

CHAPTER 19

Investment Real Estate

THERE ARE MANY do's and don'ts when it comes to investment real estate. We'd like to pass along the most important things for you to keep in mind.

Research

Before you decide to buy a foreclosed property, do the research. Ask questions of people who would provide the services that you need. Speak to a representative of your furnace company, a plumber, and/or a general contractor. After all, if you were to go on a trip, you'd probably get a bunch of maps. You'd chart your course and figure out how long it would take you to reach each stop. You'd give thought to lodging, particularly if you planned to spend more than one day in an area. You'd allow for rest stops, food stops, tolls, and maybe even road conditions.

You wouldn't sit down in your car, turn the key, and say to yourself, "I'll go north for a bit and see where it takes me, then I'll ask for further directions." If you're buying what is basically a problem property, try to get an idea of how you can address these problems before you own them.

You want to be able to react appropriately when the time comes. When we were working a lot with HUD and VA, we took a checklist with us to inspect a property. We had experience with rental management housing in ordering repairs as they were needed. We weren't construction experts, but we were able to come up with very good ballpark figures that would give a general idea of what was needed.

If you can gain entry to the property being foreclosed, you'll have a huge important advantage. If you can't get inside, an inspection of the exterior could give you an idea of what to expect. If the outside is bad, you can expect the interior to need lots of work as well.

You can tell a lot from looking at the outside of a house. You can spot rotting window frames, bad doorjambs, and roof and gutter problems. You might even be able to spot termite damage or dry rot. Of course, the driveway and walks are also spots to check.

What costs the most to repair or replace? Plumbing, heating systems, electrical systems, termite repair, and roof repair are all very expensive, not to mention repairs to basement walls. Still, you shouldn't necessarily let problems in these areas scare you away. Everything comes down to dollars: for materials, for labor, for holding time. If the dollars are all there and you still have a cushion, a safety amount in reserve, you're on the right track.

A good plumber can be a real asset in your decision-making process, as can a qualified electrician. For example, an electrician can easily give you a ballpark figure for converting to 200-amp service on a property.

Contrary to what you might think, repair of broken walls and ceilings is usually no big deal; the same holds true for tiled bathrooms that need work. Some of the most horribly vandalized properties are restored for less than you'd imagine possible. This is the reason you should not be turned off instantly by broken windows, walls, pipes, and so on. A contractor knows what's needed—even if you don't—and can order the supplies, select the proper tools, do the work, and get in and out fast. When it's all done, you'll be looking at the work of a professional, and you probably won't have paid as much as you first feared you would.

Time—It's Money and Risk to Your Property

Throughout this period, you may well be paying a high rate of interest on your loan. Taxes and insurance have to be paid, too. You want to speed things up, *really* speed them up. Your acquisition cost actually includes the interest, taxes, insurance, and related expenses incurred during the renovation. The longer it takes you to complete the job, the more it's going to cost you. (There is also the all-too-common problem of vandalism during the periods the property is empty.)

Make your own checklist; we've included one in Appendix B to use as a guide. Itemize as we've outlined and add whatever else you think is needed. If the house is occupied, figure that you may have to get a lawyer to evict, so estimate the cost of the delay and the court action. Add everything up. We again recommend including a 22 percent cushion in your totals. If you had to spend that grand total to bring the house into livable, saleable condition, would it be worth the bid price you thought you'd go to? Will it be valued at that figure by the appraiser? Would you be able to get the mortgage you need? Again, you need to know what the property is worth now and what it will be worth at the end.

Let's assume now that, armed with this information, you went to the sale and acted accordingly. Now it's your property, and your objective is to get it into condition for your occupancy, sale to others, or rental as soon as humanly possible. Of course, if you're going to move into it, you're going to put a great deal of thought into customizing your home—and once you are able to occupy, you then have the luxury of time to work with.

You may feel that a tenanted property is not at all like a home you would want to live in, that it need only be "good enough" to attract the low end of the rental market. There's a problem with this reasoning: The lower you go, the higher your risk as a landlord. If you put together a unit that will only attract renters who will take anything, whose sole goal is to get a roof over their heads, you'll pay for it in the end.

It is entirely possible that your new occupants will have a poor history as tenants. Even references from relatives or present landlords are suspect. Landlords want to get rid of people who don't pay their bills. Don't inherit someone else's problem. Bring the unit up to par. Your goal should be to attract a tenant who wants to move in, not someone who has no other choice.

Problem Tenants

We imagine we've heard just about every possible song-and-dance from bad rental risks. Here's our pick of problem cases we've learned to avoid from bitter experience.

First is the teller of tales of woe. Inexplicable bad luck seems to stalk some people wherever they go. They are very good at eliciting sympathy, very good at proving the legitimacy of the latest disaster. They're not so good at coming up with rent payments. They expect you to understand the seriousness of this week's dilemma and patiently hold off your request for rent "until this blows over." That's always at some indeterminate point in the future.

Second are the proclaimed fixer-uppers. As these prospective tenants are applying, they'll say something like, "I'm very handy; how would you feel about my making a room out of that unfinished attic up there?" You'll think it's your lucky day: A tenant is actually going to help you increase the value of your property! But it might be baloney. The potential tenant knows what you want to hear and is letting you hear it in the hope you'll ignore or overlook a bad credit record or previous problems with landlords. Often, if you scratch the surface, you'll find a deadbeat. Your tenant screening procedures must be businesslike, uniform, and include a prospective tenant credit report. Amateur hour for tenant screening makes no sense. It's the way to go only for people who don't want to sleep well.

Make sure you have legal advice on your tenant selection procedures. Your self-described handyman may tell you that he left all his personal papers with his sister/partner/whoever is in Florida or Canada or wherever and that he's going to have them mailed to him once he has an address. Or he may tell you that although he likes your place better, he'll have to take the other place he's looking at since that landlord is prepared to take him as is. There is no other place; he's trying to prey on your desire to have the unit occupied. Call the bluff. Wish him good luck and show him the door.

We urge good procedures for tenant selection because some tenants are walking disasters. Everything breaks. Everything goes wrong. You spend vast amounts of time solving problems you never expected, repairing stoves, fixing things that shouldn't have broken in the first place. Some people simply consume buildings. They devour buildings. They destroy landlords. Nobody likes hearing that, but it is so.

Many landlords know this from painful experience.

Here's another example. We know of a partnership that fixed up a twenty-eight-unit complex, supplying new kitchens, windows, aluminum storm doors, and so on. Each unit was separated by chain-link fences to protect the new landscaping. When finished, it looked like a charming little enclave, ready for occupants, where once a set of devastated buildings had been.

The tenancy was 90 percent high risk. The owners watched in disbelief as, day by day, the property disintegrated before their eyes. Within one month, the fences were torn away from the posts, the storm doors were off the hinges, the plants were ripped out, and graffiti adorned the newly painted walls. No one in the building was in any way concerned about the destruction. The partners were outraged.

Some tenants are an enormous problem—don't ask for a share. Your goal here is to identify potential problem tenants. To be sure, there are a good many low-life slumlords out there who aren't helping matters. But there are also many well-meaning individuals who start out with the belief that if you rent people a nice place to live, all of them will maintain it. Many of these well-meaning owners get hurt financially, some of them badly hurt. Many well-intentioned people lose huge amounts of money and even receive bad publicity when characterized as slumlords by reporters out to file an exciting story. We hope you don't have to go through any of that.

There are much better avenues of investment open to you if you don't want to exercise care in the selection of tenants. Remember, real estate investment carries with it the burden of real estate management. Your goal should be to make sure the burden is a manageable one.

Buying foreclosed real estate for investment property is, to many people, a way to make quick money. Given all the media on the subject, it almost looks easy. However, it is not. In this book, we describe the process clearly and truthfully. As in all efforts, one must learn the process, and there is a lot to this process.

Some readers might well conclude that the process is over their head, but many others will give it a go for a most interesting and rewarding ride. This book gives the reader a way to analyze whether he or she has what it takes to make money in buying foreclosures.

Most prospective buyers of foreclosure properties aren't trying to quit their day job; instead, they are looking for a second source of income. As a minimum, the foreclosure buyer should make at least $30,000 per property. Your profit must be much larger on higher-priced properties because your risk is much higher. And it may well take a year to realize that first profit. But once you learn the process, you can probably turn three properties a year, even as a part timer. This is not a get-rich-quick idea. It is a solid business idea.

You also must know the property values. This includes the value when you first look at a place to buy, as well as what the property will be worth if you purchase and finish it, and sell. If you do not know the values, you can get burned. One young man who paid big money for a seminar bought a fixer-upper and took a big loss on his first purchase. Why the loss?

He knew nothing about fixing property. After his loss, he approached us to locate more depressed properties to purchase.

Our statement to him was that if we located a property that made him money, he would come back for more. But if he were to lose again, we would never see him again. He didn't buy anything, and we never saw him again. He didn't know the process, territory, or values, even after dropping a few thousand dollars on a seminar and much more on his first go at an investment property. He didn't know further study and perseverance were required even after his first misstep.

CHAPTER 20

Managing Investment Real Estate

OWNING REAL PROPERTY and having tenants appeals to people looking to accumulate wealth. It is probably true that more wealth has been acquired through real estate holdings than any other medium. There is just one problem. In our years of real estate experience, we have discovered that some tenants just do not pay on time. Not only do they not pay on time, but they also create other costly problems for the property owner, problems that far outweigh the benefits.

We cannot tell you that the majority of renters are poor payers, but the number who do not pay on time are so huge that it merits an examination.

Many renters are renting only because they are not sure that they are going to remain in the area or because they would like to become acquainted with the area first and then decide where they will reside. Some of these tenants you should welcome. They are homeowners at heart and will usually treat a rental unit in the same manner that they would their home.

On the other hand, the woods are full of people who do not have the wherewithal to purchase a home. They have never been able to put aside money for anything. Owning a home is something they never expect to achieve. The first big problem is that the rent payment is the largest of their obligations. They are poor money managers, and rent is the last thing they pay each month. Meeting a due date is difficult. So they are late. In the meantime, you have been counting on that rent check in order to make your mortgage payment.

When you do not receive it on schedule, it creates a difficult situation for you. You cannot tell this to your tenant, who probably subscribes to the common belief that "Since you are a landlord, you must be rich." You will now discover that your tenant has had a particular stretch of bad luck. Not only that, he will tell you that his brother-in-law was in a terrible accident and he had to loan him his saved dollars. It is amazing how charitable and kindly these people are. They are always helping some member of their family. Of course, because you are rich, you should be able to give them a little extra time to make their rent.

As we discuss what will follow, we may appear hardhearted and unmindful of the misery in this world. But what we are sharing with you is the experiences that friends, colleagues, or we ourselves have had with real estate investments.

We attended liberal colleges. In those days, we felt very deeply about the tragedies of the poor, downtrodden masses. When we left school and recognized the necessity of working, we discovered that there are people who are winners and there are people who are losers. The caution is that when you become a landlord, you must learn to recognize those losers before they damage you. You would be better off with a three-month vacancy than accepting these people. Some of them have the capacity to destroy you.

Every now and then, your local news show will show tenants living in apartment houses with holes in the wall, garbage in the hallways, and numerous other horrible conditions. Who broke the walls? Who threw the garbage in the hallway, plus all the other indecencies? The tenants!

If you dig deeper, you may find that the owner is a plumber who saved up and had an opportunity to get what he thought was a great deal on an apartment house. He tried. He fixed. He exhausted his savings, and now in disgust he is letting the property go to foreclosure. In the meantime, the television exposé is calling him a slumlord. Do you need that kind of treatment? Do not get started with that type of tenancy. You cannot win. You are only going to go deeper into debt.

The same advice goes for purchasing a two-family house with the idea of getting the income for the rental to pay toward your mortgage. If you want a two-family to house two units of your family, that is one thing. If you are looking for the income, look at it this way: You are paying a higher price for a two-family house. In addition, the taxes are higher, so your mortgage payment is more. Now if the tenant does not pay or is slow in payment, you are living with that problem. It is an unpleasant circumstance.

Wise voices have counseled, "If you are going to be a landlord, be a big one." It is somewhat like being in a mutual fund rather than a single stock. You have a cushion against losses. But a two-family house in which you are to occupy one unit? No! No! No!

Let us get on to some tips on how you can protect yourself and help get your rent on time.

Don't rent on a verbal agreement; instead, use signed leases. They spell everything out. If you are compelled to go to court for any reason whatsoever, it is best to have the foundation of your lease agreement spelled out. If you are seeking to enforce your rights, the court will much more likely hold with you because you have a contract (the lease) and there is no other agreement. Stores that sell legal forms and some stationery stores have prepared lease forms. And of course your attorney is a far better source of a lease form, which will protect you as far as any written agreement can. It makes no sense to try and save a few hundred dollars by buying a cheap lease for a quarter- or half-million-dollar property.

Most landlords have written late charges into the agreement if the rent payment is not received on time. Some courts may question your right to levy this. Our recommendation is this. Let's say that you want to get a rental amount of $950. Offer the unit at $1,000. You tell your prospective tenants "I must explain that the rental is $1,000 and my lease will state that amount. I will, however, have the following clause in the lease: Provided that the rental payment is received by 5:00 P.M. on the fifth day of each month, the tenant will be granted a discount of $50 with such payment."

The difference is that you have an agreement for $1,000.

A word of caution is needed in reviewing prospective clients' credit reports. If there is no record available on a person well past his early years, you could very well have been given a false social security number. If the applicant claims to have never had credit experience, say no. Do not go that route unless you are a glutton for punishment and financial loss.

Checking references is another caution. Personal references have a limited value. What about his previous landlord? Well, that landlord may be anxious to get rid of that tenant, so the landlord will not give you any adverse reports.

You have to be the psychologist. As mentioned, if your prospective tenant is offering to improve your property in some way, your antennae should go up. It should make you want to check him much more closely. He is giving you the romance. We know. We were taken in by that ruse the first time that we encountered such a generous soul. If you do a drive-by of your prospective tenant's current address, you might be able to get an idea of how he is going to treat your property.

If you come across an adverse credit report, do not think that you can compensate by taking an additional security deposit. When you have a bad experience with a tenant, you will find that the wheels of justice grind slowly and your time buffer disintegrates.

Should your lease commence after the first day of the month, calculate the amount for the partial month and have the full amount due on the first of every month thereafter. It is much better for your bookkeeping.

The person who tells you that he just moved into town may be telling you the truth. Look at his license plates. Are they from out of state, as claimed? Prospective tenants include experienced con artists.

Spend some time exploring tenant screening procedures before it is time to rent out your place. Your city may have a building owners' and managers' organization. Spending eight to twenty hours learning these ropes before you act will really pay off.

Remember once you have surrendered your premises to an individual, you are in your weakest position. You can only remove a tenant through due process of law, and that can be time consuming and frustrating, and it can cost you quite a few bucks.

If you need to resort to legal process, you may meet someone else you wish you could have avoided: your tenant's attorney. You may now be served with an "order to show cause." This is almost always nothing more than a stalling tactic used by the legal beagles to give their clients time to find some other poor soul who will turn over their well-kept property to these disruptive tenants.

You will now discover that (according to the complaint) there is no water, no fuel (if you provide it), a broken stove, and so on. This is your first notice that anything was wrong with the premises. Deficiencies almost always occur after you start your eviction. Fortunately, the judges are aware of this device, and eventually you will get your tenants out. But this has a cost in lost rent and additional legal expenses.

Have we made our point clear? You cannot change some people. Not only do they not respect property, they see landlords as the enemy who is out to suck their blood. Is this an overstatement? Some tenants have voiced these sentiments many times.

Invest in real estate, but make sure that you have investigated your prospective tenants' records. Get a good tenant, and you will enjoy the fruits of your investment. Good luck!

CHAPTER 21

Those Easy-Money, No-Cash Commercials and Seminars

FREE SEMINAR on How to Make Money on Foreclosures. Free Workshop. Hurry, Space Is Limited. Hurry! *Free.*

Real estate seminar ads may use other words. But we have all seen the beckoning ads on foreclosure seminars or for real estate acquisition programs, often implying great rewards with little or no cash or experience required.

In the real estate sales business, *free* seminars are readily available, especially in the winter, when sales are down in much of the country. So what is the hook? The *free* seminar is a *free* sales presentation to a room full of sales agents who are looking for a way to improve their business. The last part of the *free* seminar is a closing pitch to sell their written sales system. If you walk out without putting your money down, it was *free.*

If you walk out with an armful of materials and a credit card receipt, it wasn't *free.* Free foreclosure seminars work on the same model. That model is almost always a no-cash purchase.

Let's take a realistic look at a no-cash purchase. Who is going to sell you a property with no money down? What is actually meant by "free" in this context is "none of *your* money down." In this scenario, you borrow the down payment as well as the rest of the purchase price. Sure, it sounds great, especially if you have no cash. But in the real world, such deals often involve prohibitively high interest rates or some other catch. However, there is one way to have success when you've got little cash to work with.

If you have home improvement skills, such as carpentry, electrical, or plumbing experience, and you know the building codes, you might want to partner with a real estate agent who does have cash. That agent might well want to put up the down payment and materials money if you agree to do all the labor, then split any profit.

A real estate agent has access to property information, knows how to buy and finance and how to sell, and knows valuation at the start and at the end of the project. After doing a couple of properties in a partnership, you might well decide to go on your own. Or you might fare much better sticking with the partnership. We would recommend staying with what works. And a written partnership agreement is the way to go. It doesn't need to be greatly detailed if it covers all the basics and most possible outcomes.

In any no-cash deal, you must provide something. Your labor might well be that something. Otherwise, a purchase on your own will require a first mortgage on the property and usually a second mortgage on your present home. And that's a very bad idea. However, if you are going to live in the property you are buying, 100 percent financing and going it alone could be acceptable to you. If you then need to sell your present home, you must have a realistic sense of the price needed to sell quickly. In some markets, that price will be shockingly low.

Now let's consider buying for investment. You look to find a tenant for something approaching monthly payment, taxes, insurance, and maintenance. Even if you are lucky enough to find that tenant, just remember, one month's vacancy could wipe you out. So you might as well face the facts: No-cash deals are risky! And you will be carrying that risk until you sell, in the absence of huge property appreciation.

Here is the real deal. If the transaction you are contemplating doesn't pass the sniff test, it probably is sour. If it doesn't pass the common sense test, it probably is no good. Use common sense in this. The stakes for you with 100 percent financing are huge. You are rolling the dice with your financial future.

Before World War II, America was a country of renters. With the GI Bill and the establishment of the FHA, the real estate market opened up. A veteran could buy a house with no cash down, and an FHA buyer could buy with only 3 percent down. They still can.

House hunting became a national pastime. One great advantage of those mortgages was that they could be transferred to a new buyer with no credit check of the buyer. As time went on and more houses were sold subject to the existing mortgage (mortgage assumptions), lenders found themselves boxed in with low-interest-rate mortgages. New mortgages were being offered at higher rates, and so many buyers at that time, even those with good credit, sought out homes being sold with existing VA or FHA mortgages. Well, the "good old days of assumable loans" are long gone, and due-on-sale clauses are the rule.

A first-time buyer called informing us that he had just bought a place on a land contract, and he didn't need us to search for properties for him anymore. After a couple of questions, we learned that there was a first mortgage on the place he was trying to buy. Figure it out. Can that seller sell his place on a land contract if there is an existing mortgage? Of course not. You can't put another first lien on a property if a first lien (mortgage) already exists. The seller can't sell without lender approval. We tried to give the buyer advice on this, and explained that the first mortgage has first lien position, and a land contract is an event triggering the due-on-sale clause.

However, after a couple of minutes, we could tell that the buyer would not listen to our advice, so we gave him the name of an attorney. We said our advice was free, but that the attorney would charge a bunch. Go for it. We bet he didn't. Another case of somebody chasing something for nothing! Many seminars take advantage of that same desire to get something for nothing. It looks like the easy way, and everyone wants an easy way. That's why there are so many TV commercials for the easy way to lose weight, the easy way to make money, and on and on and on.

Seminars

Let's look at it this way. There are thousands of practicing real estate brokers, agents, and attorneys in this country. They typically know more about real estate than the general public. Why aren't they sitting in the front row of these seminars and out there buying up these properties before you get there? Figure it out.

Many of the real estate offerings advertised in these seminars are absolutely worthless or worse. What does an owner have to lose if he actually could buy with no money down and then rent the property as an investment? If tenants trash the place and break everything in sight (and some do), the owner can walk away and let the lender take over. After all, the owner has no money at risk, while the supplier of the money, the lender, has all of the risk. No heat, no electricity, no maintenance. When the owner walks away who will maintain the place? The tenants could contact Legal Aid. Legal Aid might get a judge to order the owner or even the lender to provide services.

Just think. The lender might not own the property, but it may end up with owner's responsibilities. The last thing the lender may want is ownership of the building. But the lender may be saddled with lender responsibilities and all the problems that go with it, including bad news tenants, and still not be in title or able to sell. The same kind of upside-down position and inability to sell can come the way of the borrower owner; that is, she might find herself under a court-ordered obligation to spend even more money on continuing repairs on a bad-news property that is already a huge money pit. How would you like to be stuck with that?

Maybe you can change the tenants. Maybe, like a young woman who contemplates marrying a man who is a cheat, a philanderer, a manipulator, and who is probably also a liar. With no cash down, you have at least as much chance as she does of changing that fellow. On a post-foreclosure lender-owned property, let's assume the lender is willing to provide a buyer extremely favorable financing. The lender is both making purchase easy for a buyer but also signaling a great willingness to no longer own that property. The property may be a real dog, which howls in the night with problems a buyer may not spot until too late.

You may be advised to borrow against an income property you own or even against your residence. Let's assume you borrow using a home equity loan. It provides for payments to be made at a reasonably agreeable rate. Now you can get a mortgage from a lender, for the balance of the new purchase price, or maybe even seller financing. Here is where things can backfire.

Now you have 100 percent debt. As long as properties appreciate substantially, the percentage of debt decreases, but what happens in the case of a flat or declining market? A pyramid of cards can collapse and collapse quickly. When things are good in the real estate market and values are climbing steadily, you cannot make a mistake, and you will be flying high. When prices stall or fold, 100 percent debt can devour you.

Now let's take a final look at the world of the free workshop and the free seminar. Having been commission salesmen for decades, and having attended more than a few "free" seminars, we can predict the format:

- The speakers must have an audience, so they place newspaper ads or send out mailers targeting the audience they want. The majority of the attendees are looking for something for nothing, so the word "free" catches them. That's why they attend.

- The "workshop seminar" is actually a sales presentation to sell a future workshop or seminar. The "free" presentation is simply a survey of things to come. Sometimes the subsequent workshop or seminars or even the first seminar is marketing the presenters' sales system.
- The presentations are given by very fluent and convincing speakers. They want to play into that old human desire to get something for nothing.
- The presenters give a price for the real workshop (seminar) and a detailed explanation of how inexpensive it is (spread out over a year and subtracted from increased income during that year). They make it sound free.
- Then comes the close. "If you sign today, we will give you a $1,000 discount, $4,000 minus $1,000, tax deductible because it probably can be an education expense." "If you pass on this today, you will be denying your family all that money."

Does the seminar system actually work? Yes, especially for those who operate the seminars. Their revenues can be surprisingly large. However, they are quite effective for a few types of individuals. Some of us are better learners with hands-on training than we are by self study. For those types, the seminar might be the only way to gain a lot of knowledge. But not for most.

Now, if you attend a seminar, at least you know in advance to either take your credit card along or to leave it at home.

Personality and Aptitude Matters

Now that you understand how the seminar world works, it is important for you to assess whether you can weave through the process of buying foreclosures on your own, such as by studying this book, or whether you need personal training by others. Some individuals are astute at going on their own, while others must have hands-on personal instruction. Of course, hands-on training requires someone else's time, so you must be prepared to pay for it.

Let's take a look at personality and some of the mechanics that play into this decision:

- Would you feel comfortable in telephone or face-to-face meetings with lender officers, mortgage servicing officers, real estate brokers, attorneys, and others in your search for properties?
- Can you prepare professional-looking letters or proposals?
- Are you proficient at Internet searching?

Professional people are accustomed to dealing with people who behave like them, who dress like them, and who talk like them. Typically, they are not comfortable dealing with someone who doesn't. So if you're going to go into this field, you must be prepared to dress, talk, and behave like a professional. Only you can determine if you're comfortable doing that.

Let's assume that it will take twenty-five personal contacts to locate the property you want, and let's assume that property will generate a profit of $30,000 within three months. We can set up the formula like so: Profit (in this case, $30,000) divided by the number of contacts (here, 25) equals the value of each contact. In this example, the value of every contact is $1,200. It took twenty-four various kinds of disappointments to get one property. That's a lot of disappointment. But shrewd investors know that it takes time, training, and persistence to find what they're looking for. If you're discouraged by a run of disappointments, just keep telling yourself: If I make $30,000 on this property and it takes me twenty-five disappointments to get there, each disappointment is actually putting me $1,200 closer to my goal.

That may lessen the disappointment.

PART THREE

The Road Ahead

CHAPTER 22

Fear and Greed

YOU MAY THINK that's a funny title for a book chapter. Yet an understanding of fear and its bedfellow, greed, and how big a part of conventional wisdom they are in finance—and particularly in the national and local real estate markets—is necessary. That understanding is absolutely essential if we hope to make good decisions about buying foreclosed real estate.

Let's take a quick tour of the Land of Fear. This isn't "someone-is-coming-at-me-right-now-with-an-axe" fear but rather a widely held financial fear: Specifically, it's the fear of a bear market on Wall Street. Enough people have direct or indirect stock ownership for this fear to be held by millions. Bear markets on Wall Street mean plunging stock prices—prices that are down for days, down for weeks, resulting in bad months, bad quarters, and sometimes even longer periods of sharply dropping stock prices. All of that affects and is affected by the state of the real estate market. It can make a big difference in your decision to purchase or to pass on a deal. What can trigger a bear market? Here are a few of the most common factors:

- Substantial negative financial information
- Minor negative financial information

- Minor positive financial information
- Substantial positive financial information
- No financial information
- Headline events such as the September 11, 2001, terrorist attacks

How can you understand the stock market? First, it helps to know what causes bear markets and to recognize how unpredictable some of the causes can be. It also helps to know that most bear markets can be recognized after they occur or while they are occurring much better than they can be predicted. True enough, negative events are somewhat more likely to be bear-market triggers, but negative events aren't required.

Don't think so? Let's look at just one period of time. Let's use the dot-com boom and bust. And let's just look at the NASDAQ, where most of it occurred. First, let's identify the underlying cause of the dot-com boom: substantial positive financial information that the growing use of the Internet provided many efficiencies of operation and many business opportunities for new firms willing to ride the dot-com boom.

And what caused the dot-com bust? Again, it was substantial positive financial information that the growing use of the Internet provides many efficiencies of operation and many business opportunities for new firms willing to ride the dot-com boom.

Aside from the fact that either a boom or bust was occurring, were the overall underlying economic conditions of the United States appreciably different in the last two months of the boom compared to the first two months of the bust? Were the financial prospects of the dot-coms appreciably different in the last two months of the boom compared to the first two months of the bust? The answer to both questions is no. All that happened was that an increasing number of venture capitalists recognized the flawed business models of the dot-coms they were backing and cut off their funding. As word spread throughout the financial community, fear of losses spread, and the movement snowballed. Economic conditions didn't change; perceptions did.

At work on the way up for those venture capitalists had been the fear of missing a sweet chance to make a lot of money. On the way down, they were driven by fear as well: fear of *losing* a lot of money.

Make sense? Logical? No. Completely bizarre behavior for a bunch of bright people? Fear can be a very compelling emotion.

What else could have been the trigger that turned the dot-com boom into a bust? Did price/earnings ratios change? Did general economic conditions change? Or did fear drive the dot-com market lower in just a few short weeks, just as fear of missing a nice ride on the way up had made the market rise just a few months earlier?

We'd like to think that something more knowledgeable, more informed, more intelligent than fear drove the dot-com rocket upward or pushed it downward into a crash. Maybe we need to give fear its place of honor (or dishonor) when we look at major stock market swings.

Now let's turn to the major real estate downturn that began in mid-2005. Did underlying rents or real estate taxes change dramatically? Did our population suddenly stop growing? Of course not. Divorces, death, marriage, more kids, old age infirmity, unemployment rate, employment transfers, and all the other reasons for buying continued as before. Did rising interest rates (rates still moderate by the standards of recent decades) make it undesirable to own real estate? Did prices escalate so dramatically that only the lucky folks who owned real estate that could be sold had enough money to buy? Did unemployment soar, or did the economy go into recession? Not at all.

Many people in 2003 and 2004 assumed real estate prices would continue to rise indefinitely. Afraid of missing out on a boom, they invested heavily. In the same way, by mid-2007, many people assumed real estate prices in most of the United States would be flat or declining for the foreseeable future. Again, there was plenty of fear on the way down over the present and future value of real estate, fear that in a very large proportion of the country, real estate couldn't be sold except at a large discount.

Fear as an economic motivator has a buddy. They're a great team. If one of them is resting, the other is usually working. Fear's good buddy is greed.

Greed has a bad name. It deserves better. It needs to be treated as a five-letter word. The gush of money that drove the Great Real Estate Boom was driven in part by greed. That story is worth reading—if for no other reason than because understanding it can mean personally avoiding the downside of the next hot investment fashion, in which everybody is once again trying to make money.

Greed drives all kinds of money decisions. It is a huge motivating force. It was a big reason Americans settled and developed our land from the Atlantic to the Pacific Ocean. It is maybe the biggest motivating cause we have. It helps to get us up in the mornings and off to work. But greed is color blind. It doesn't play favorites. It can induce some of our best economic decisions, lead to brilliant investment choices, and also to super business and personal financial moves.

It can also lead to bad choices, bad moves, and even to financial disaster. Greed can induce hard work and great sacrifices and can lead the way to accumulating great sums of money and even great wealth. It can also push people into following the latest investment fad and losing tons of money. Greed is powerful and can be a help in getting people to their financial goal. But it can fall upon the greedy like a gang of thieves and take their money and treasure as surely as if they were plundered at sword point.

Greed doesn't drive all human endeavors or motivate all people. But it drives many, sometimes most, of our economic decisions. Along with its buddy, fear, it can drive an economy to boom and bust and back time and again. Staying away from real estate now? Are you doing it because that's the correct personal decision about a super property in a great location? Or are you reacting to the fear that real estate is in free-fall and everyone knows it? Investors have to understand what part of our decisions about real estate purchases are driven by rational consideration of all the pluses and minuses and what part is driven by those primitive but very powerful emotions, fear and greed.

It's hard to separate out the accepted conventional wisdom from a well-thought-out individual decision based on all available information. But it's the best way to go when it comes to a major economic or money decision like decisions about real estate. And if investors fully understand and are honest about fear and greed, they will be much more likely to make the best financial decisions.

Here's Another Big Help— Knowing Another Way Decisions Are Made

It's the weekend, and you're looking at a decision about a particular real estate matter. You've gathered and analyzed all relevant information. You've analyzed the role fear can play. You've done the same with greed. You think you're ready to decide. It might be good to know what psychologist Gordon W. Alport told his Harvard students many decades ago. He believed that humans make many—maybe most—of their decisions by selecting the option that minimizes their stress and anxiety.

If the professor is correct, this doesn't sound like a good way to decide. The decision with minimal stress and anxiety could easily be a terrible decision. It's not driven by logic, not even by sorting information. But if Alport's theory is on target, it's an extremely good thing to keep in mind when figuring out not only what we've decided but why we decided what we did. Bottom line: The more we know about how we and others make decisions, the better decisions we will make.

CHAPTER 23

Fine-Tuning Your Thinking

WHEN THINKING OF buying financially distressed property, you must make sure your pricing decisions fully reflect the present and potential stresses on real estate prices in your market. Remember to keep an eye on the regional and national real estate market. As for most property, local, regional, and national market trends will have very much to do with how well you fare on all your real estate moves, whether you are purchasing, selling, or standing pat.

Will the real estate market be back? Certainly. Is there more downside danger? Darn right. Some markets will remain very weak for a long time. But there are many chances to acquire property that will look like a brilliant move in a surprisingly short time.

Do you think the foreclosed property you are thinking about buying will go up in value or that it will go down? As we wrote before, you must know the numbers. If you don't have a very good idea of the present value and the future value of a property, you will not buy.

If you don't know the numbers on your own, it is imperative that you team with or hire someone who does.

Also, you must use your own initiative to find foreclosed properties. Every locality is different, and there are different personalities to deal with. In some localities, the local clerk might be helpful, but in others that person might be of no help at all. Each market is different.

We say that it is critical to have a team on your side. Your team should include the following members:

- A real estate broker or an appraiser to get the numbers
- An attorney and title company to get the title and legal aspects right
- A contractor or rehab person to give you good estimates for repair and upgrade

We feel if you follow this advice, you will make the right decisions. If you try buying without knowing the numbers, you won't.

Here's an important bit of advice for all your real estate and major financial decisions. Approach your financial analysis as much as you can with the attitude that "I'm taking it from the top here because I'm new in town and unfamiliar with the type of investment I'm looking at." Then factor back in all your previous knowledge, including your previous biases, partialities, preconceptions, and even your prejudices and prejudgments. Weigh it all together, and make your final decision.

Finance Fashions

Along the way, of course, you'll run into a lot of advice from other people—some good, some bad. One thing to beware of, though, is getting sucked into the latest investing fad or shaken by the latest popular crisis.

Here are some of the more recent ones:

- Oil patch loans
- Latin American loans
- The savings-and-loan crisis
- The Asian markets crisis
- The dot-com boom and bust
- Subprime mortgages
- Enron
- MCI
- Junk bonds

It's a long list. Longer than we'd like. This one is certainly not all-inclusive, and it is all relatively recent history. How do intelligent people get sucked into these things? Is investing just gambling?

After keeping a close watch on real estate and real estate finance over several decades, we believe these fads have common elements:

- A desire for above-average returns
- A willingness to rely too much on conventional wisdom
- Chasing the current hot investment fashion

In short, it pays to stay away from a lot of these hot new trends. Before you jump into the Next Big Thing, you must at the very least analyze the reasons for entering the market. Include the factors of fear and greed in your calculations, and assemble as much information as possible. That way, you'll be able to avoid getting caught up in the latest finance fashion and keep your investments profitable.

CHAPTER 24

We Didn't Know
Mortgages and Real Estate
Were That Important

THE YEAR 2007 BEGAN with the U.S. economy performing quite well; unemployment rates were at the lower end of their historic range, and economic growth, while generally thought to be slowing, was still continuing a long expansion. Despite high and rising oil prices, inflation numbers were far from bad. Recession was considered only a small possibility, with consumer spending holding up. Stock markets were beginning a nice run. And while the continuing slide of the dollar was noted by some, only a continuing sideways or downward move in most residential real estate prices, along with many spikes in foreclosures plus very rough sledding for builders, were obvious minuses.

But by mid-year, the new phrases *subprime mortgages* and *subprime lending*, first heard the previous year, were common. By late summer almost everyone had heard of or ridden the bumpy road of stock market volatility.

In market terms, *volatility* translates into "some really bad days." By spring, some subprime lenders, including the nation's largest subprime lender, New Century, had been completely crushed. Other mid-sized and large mortgage lending firms ceased operation. The list got longer and longer.

By August, the cages of financial firms around the world, more highly leveraged firms of all types, and even the most solid firms with little or absolutely no mortgage business had been well rattled. Any reader of the financial and popular press could find foreclosure, real estate price, subprime lending, and mortgage articles in the hundreds. And those really bad days of big declines in stock prices were hard for anyone to miss.

Most ominous for real estate prices in the United States was the widespread disappearance of purchasers of mortgages and the disappearance of institutional private equity and hedge-fund buyers of subprime mortgages (except those buying at discounts of more than 50 percent).

There was the heavy shaking of the major financial market for mortgage loans and the decimation, the collapse of its significant sub-market, subprime lending. It didn't take much thinking to see the contagion could spread to other credit markets and industries, and then to all but the strongest of borrowers, with a following general economic crumble.

Before the U.S. markets opened for the day on August 17, 2007, the U.S. Federal Reserve acknowledged that "the downside risks to growth have increased appreciably" and further said it would "act as needed to mitigate the adverse effects on the economy arising from the disruptions in financial markets." The Fed lowered the discount rate of relatively little used and somewhat stigmatized overnight loans to banks and extended the term of those loans to as much as thirty days. On September 18, 2007, the Fed followed up with a 0.5 drop in both the discount and Fed funds interest rates.

The Fed action and its announcement of its willingness to take further action "as needed," along with its previous moves in coordination with other central banks of massive liquidity injections just before September 17, seemed to prevent the kind of financial market meltdown of which nightmares and great widespread intense economic pain are made.

Also, on August 31, 2007, President Bush offered a welcome but modest program to assist some borrowers facing foreclosure with more liberal terms than previously available on FHA loans for borrowers in need of refinancing. More importantly to many, the president recommended changing the U.S. tax code so that the amount of lender renegotiation negotiated to favor distressed borrowers is no longer treated as taxable income. It is unlikely that this proposal would have been made if substantial and continued really rough times for challenged borrowers and real estate prices were not expected. In September, the White House leaned toward expanding FMNA and FHLMC lending authority after initially opposing any expansion. This action was a response to deteriorating real estate market conditions.

Nonetheless, real estate and other investors will likely long remember the August dance at the edge. They will remember the uncertainty about the wisdom of holding real estate or real estate debt for a long time. Builders and developers will for years be unwilling to step forward as briskly with the pounding of nails or the subdivision of new parcels of land. Municipalities will show considerably more caution in their approval process steps. And lenders will be much slower and more restrictive in funding even yesterday's slam-dunk loans. Years of below-population-growth building will ultimately self-correct most real estate markets.

The entire field of private-fund investing will have redefining reviews, some ugly losses and failures, and maybe even a total renaming for hedge funds by those who operate them. (After all, the savings-and-loan debacle of the 1980s caused an institutional name change, from "S&L" to "savings banks.")

Private-fund investing will also have some nice opportunities and performances as hunts for the next hot investment slow and the quality of analysis and decision-making improves. Either way, even some real estate markets overseas will likely see some reductions in rates of price increases and actual price declines.

There are many factors mitigating against a return of boom-like conditions in most U.S. cities. For example, the loss of subprime lending options for the bottom 10 percent of purchasers, the discouragement of the next 10 percent to even apply for financing, and a huge conventional-wisdom swing against real estate in most markets will weigh heavily on real estate prices for years, even decades in the absence of quite a few Fed reductions in short-term interest rates.

These reductions may well not occur given inflationary pressures and the already strongly eroded condition of the U.S. dollar.

Ironically, a sharp recession with its origins in the decline of real estate values may induce the kind of Fed moves to cause real estate to ultimately again lead the way, this time in a much happier direction.

Remember that powerful conventional wisdom, which holds that a decline of real estate prices is needed before general price stabilization. Once this happens, we're told, a general increase in prices will occur in most markets. Whether or not this happens remains to be seen, but you sure now know what to look for.

And foreclosure and workout opportunities (post-, preforeclosure, and on the auction block) will continue to be more numerous than in the years of boom. Likewise, there will be plenty of economic loss for those transactions too dependent on a fictional continuous upward climb in real estate prices.

The need for, and the value of, making good real estate decisions will never be greater than in the coming years. You'll do well because we walked the same real estate route together.

Our best regards go with you.

T.D.

D.A.

D.P.

Frequently Asked Questions

Following are answers to some of the most commonly posed questions regarding purchases of foreclosures and related issues.

Q. *Are there closing costs when buying a property at foreclosure sale?*

A. Yes: the cost of the title insurance policy and the cost of recording your deed. Other costs may occur in some places. And of course the cost of borrowed money (or lost income, if you use your own funds) is real.

Q. *Will I need a lawyer when buying a property at foreclosure sale?*

A. There's really not much a lawyer can do for you at the sale itself. The terms are set; the lawyer will not be able to change them. Your title insurance commitment and policy is the best protection as to the title you receive. Your attorney *can* provide invaluable information and advice so you are well armed with knowledge before you finalize your real estate decisions such as bidding at a foreclosure sale.

Q. *Once you put your bid in at the foreclosure sale, can the homeowner still get the property back before you put down the balance?*

A. No. Once the sale goes forth and is confirmed, it is final in all but the rarest of cases.

Q. *I'm concerned about the permanence of the foreclosure sale I'm contemplating. Doesn't the former owner have the right to buy the house back within a year?*

A. That's what's known as a "right of redemption." Such rights do not exist in foreclosure sales having already expired in most jurisdictions although they often do in tax sales or sheriff's sales. See the earlier chapters on foreclosure sales and tax sales for more information on these transactions. You'll want the advice of your attorney before you spend or commit to spend money in any real estate matter. We do.

Q. *How do you get people out of the property if they continue to occupy after the sale? Won't the lender take care of that?*

A. The lender will not handle this for you. You'll have to go to court. This situation is similar to a tenant holdover conflict in which a landlord wishes to eject a tenant from a rental property. You'll need the marshal or sheriff, whichever your county uses, to remove the occupants legally after a court orders their removal. This could be difficult in a rent-controlled area. Again, have the advice of your attorney.

Q. *Can I get a VA loan on a foreclosure?*

A. Not on a foreclosed property bought at public auction. You must pay in full within thirty days; you cannot buy the property with a financing contingency. Such sales are "all cash," although you might be able to get a VA mortgage on a lender-owned property sold pre- or post-foreclosure.

Q. *Why shouldn't lenders look forward to selling out properties with small mortgages so they can make money on the sale?*

A. Acquired real estate is something lenders would rather not have on their financial statements. They'd much prefer to have these properties sold to third parties and generally sustain losses, often big-time losses. At a foreclosure sale, lenders are not entitled to any surplus over what is owed them and what they expend to protect the property and complete the foreclosure.

Q. *I've gone to a house that was in the process of being foreclosed, but the occupant wouldn't let me in to see the place. How can I get a look before placing a bid?*

A. If you were in the other person's shoes, you wouldn't want to let anyone in, either. You may be limited to an exterior assessment. On the other hand, if the house is vacant, you can always try calling the lender. You may get in for a look; after all, the lender wants to sell the property.

Q. *Where can I learn about properties being foreclosed?*

A. If there is no business publication in your area that covers these matters, you can go to the county courthouse where the foreclosure notices are posted. Also look through the newspaper designated for official legal notices. You will find public notices there.

Q. *Where are foreclosure sales held?*

A. The notice of foreclosure sale will indicate where the sale will be held. Typically, sales are held on the steps of the courthouse. As noted earlier in this book, when the notice states that the sale will be held "on the courthouse steps," it really does mean the physical outdoor steps leading into the building. If you are confused about location, call ahead or ask security personnel for help. You must be prompt in arriving at foreclosure sales.

Q. *Let's assume that I am the successful bidder at the sale. Am I obligated to pay up any other creditors of the party being foreclosed?*

A. Rely on your attorney and the title insurance company. Also remember to inquire about taxes before you bid.

Q. *Suppose that a second mortgage is being foreclosed and that I win the bid. Do I have to pay up the first mortgage completely?*

A. You want to know this before you bid. Many lenders will exercise their due on sale rights. Ask your legal eagle for recommendations. Many lenders will want to exercise their acceleration option and call the full balance due.

Q. *If I win the bid and someone turns up with a legitimate claim on the property, do I have to pay it?*

A. If by "legitimate," you mean that the claim precedes the foreclosing party's claim bid and was missed on the title search, the answer is no—as long as you have title insurance. The title insurance company is on the hook for such a claim. This scenario is one example of what you are paying to avoid when you buy title insurance.

Q. *Will the lender put in a new stove? Reupholster the furniture? Fix the neglect of the past owner?*

A. All of these "will the lender" questions—and many others—aren't likely to be answered the way you'd hope. The lender won't do anything to property it doesn't own except board it up to prevent vandalism. If you buy a previously foreclosed property from the lender's acquired real estate, that's a different story. In such a case, the lender owns the property.

You can ask for anything. What you get will depend on the lender's response to your request. However, you may be better served by reducing your offer price and having the work done for you after you acquire title.

Q. If a property is being foreclosed, could I arrange to buy it before the sale from the owner and continue his mortgage?

A. If you could get an agreement for a deed from the mortgagor, you could talk to the lender about reinstating the mortgage and assuming it. If you're a good credit risk, you may be able to pull this off. But remember, all negotiation with an owner under financial distress is challenging and in the end still subject to owner second thoughts and backing out and even later contesting what was first agreed to. Keep your attorney's phone number handy. Important: Make sure there is no other recorded debt against the property.

Q. I'd like to simplify things. Is there a rule of thumb to help me determine what percentage of value I should pay for a foreclosure?

A. No. Too many variables—condition, salability, location, financing, and taxes, to name only a few—come into play.

Q. My state has very favorable mortgage rates for a first-time buyer, and I'd like to take advantage of them. If I buy in at the foreclosure sale, can I then apply for the first-time buyer's rate?

A. Unfortunately, the answer here is probably not what you want to hear. If you buy at the sale and use your line of credit or personal assets to take title, subsequently you're refinancing and will usually not be considered a first-time buyer. Note: You may want to look into the possibility of having a relative make the purchase as income property and then buy it from that person with your own financing. This may be easier than you think if your relative is willing to use a home equity loan for the purpose of financing this relatively brief transaction.

Q. *If the foreclosed property has improvements that were never finally inspected and there are no certificates of occupancy for them, will the lender furnish these certificates at the sale?*

A. No. This is one of the perils of buying a foreclosure. In order to get a permanent mortgage loan on the property, you may have to get the certificates. This is usually not a major setback, but you will have to do some legwork and handle the expenses associated with the process and possibly additional contractor work if the municipality so requires.

Q. *I have a friend who's a plumber; he'll inspect, for free, the house I have my eye on. Can I bring him into any house I want to bid on?*

A. If the people in possession will let you in, yes. If they won't, no. The current occupants are under no obligation to permit you to inspect.

Q. *What are the rights of tenants under a lease?*

A. It depends on the particulars of your situation. Seek legal advice.

Q. *I've heard that real estate brokers have an inside track on the good foreclosures. Is this true?*

A. The only edge they have is their knowledge of the market. They will probably recognize a good buy before someone unfamiliar with the real estate environment in which they work.

Q. *I've heard that novice buyers sometimes face a stacked deck when attempting to buy foreclosed properties from the lender. Is this true? Do lenders show favoritism toward certain bidders at an auction sale?*

A. Foreclosure sales are conducted by a designated party acting in official capacity and who is obligated to act with impartiality. Exceptions to impartial conduct are very rare. If the lender already owns the property, it is different. Lenders want to sell to buyers they know can write the check and close quickly. If your offer to buy from the lender is professional and convincing in appearance, you have a very good chance.

Q. *If the prior owner didn't pay the taxes on a foreclosed property, does the successful bidder have to pay them?*

A. No. But if the taxes aren't paid, the county can sell the property out from under the lender's mortgage lien. Lenders usually pay the amounts due to municipalities and sell the property with all tax payments current.

Q. *How does a tax sale differ from a foreclosure sale?*

A. In many jurisdictions, when the public authorities offer a property for sale to satisfy a tax lien, the successful bidder buys the right to own the property if the property owner does not repay the bidder. This is not the case at a foreclosure sale.

Checklists

Take this checklist with you when you examine a property. See if you can estimate what is needed; allow yourself a reasonable figure to accomplish whatever must be done. Estimate high, and then give yourself an additional 22 percent cushion.

EXTERIOR	
Item	*Estimated Cost*
Driveway, walks	$
Shrubbery, lawn	$
Rubbish removal	$
Screens and storm windows	$
Chimney	$
Window repair	$
Front door	$
Front storm door	$
Rear door	$
Rear storm door	$
Garage door	$
Screened porch	$
Patio	$
Front stoop	$
Rear stoop	$
Siding/shingles repair	$
Fascia repair	$
Roof repair	$
Other	$
Total	$

Notes: _____

_____

_____

_____

INTERIOR		
	LIVING ROOM	**DINING ROOM**
Item	*Estimated Cost*	*Estimated Cost*
Floor repair	$	$
Carpeting	$	$
Moldings	$	$
Walls	$	$
Closet doors	$	$
Electrical outlets	$	$
Electrical fixtures	$	$
Air conditioner	$	$
Heating fixtures	$	$
Thermostat	$	$
Other	$	$
Other	$	$
Other	$	$
Other	$	$
Other	$	$
Other	$	$
Other	$	$
Other	$	$
Total	$	$

Notes: _____

_____

_____

_____

INTERIOR		
	KITCHEN	BATHROOM
Item	*Estimated Cost*	*Estimated Cost*
Floor	$	$
Walls	$	$
Cabinets	$	$
Sink	$	$
Stove	$	
Commode		$
Electrical outlets	$	$
Electrical fixtures	$	$
Appliance repair/replacement	$	
Tub/shower		$
Heating fixtures	$	$
Other	$	$
Other	$	$
Other	$	$
Other	$	$
Other	$	$
Other	$	$
Other	$	$
Total	$	$

Notes: _____

_____

_____

_____

INTERIOR			
BEDROOMS			
MASTER	SECOND	THIRD	FOURTH
Item	Estimated Cost		
Floors	$	$	$	$
Walls	$	$	$	$
Closet doors	$	$	$	$
Moldings, trim	$	$	$	$
Electrical outlets	$	$	$	$
Electrical fixtures	$	$	$	$
Air conditioner	$	$	$	$
Heating fixtures	$	$	$	$
Thermostat	$	$	$	$
Other	$	$	$	$
Other	$	$	$	$
Other	$	$	$	$
Other	$	$	$	$
Other	$	$	$	$
Other	$	$	$	$
Other	$	$	$	$
Other	$	$	$	$
Total	$	$	$	$

Notes: _____

_____

_____

_____

BASEMENT	
Item	*Estimated Cost*
Stairs	$
Floor	$
Walls	$
Electrical outlets	$
Electrical fixtures	$
Heating unit	$
Hot water unit	$
Air conditioner	$
Plumbing repairs	$
Water lines	$
Oil tank	$
Other	$
Total	$

PAINTING	
Item	*Estimated Cost*
Exterior	$
Interior	$
Total	$

Notes: _____

_____

_____

_____

Overall Total Cost of Repair and Renovation	$

OVERALL COST OF PURCHASE	
Item	*Estimated Cost*
Bid price	$
Acquisition costs	$
Holding costs	$
Repairs and renovations	$
Cost of Money $_____ @ _____% interest	$
Sales costs	$
Total cost of purchase and sale	$

PROFIT	
Item	*Estimated Cost*
Ultimate sale price	$
Less total costs	$
Anticipated profit	$

ANALYSIS	
Sale price in renovated condition	$

COST OF SALE	
Item	*Estimated Cost*
Commission	$
Legal fees	$
Stamps on deed	$
Preparation of mortgage	$
Satisfaction	$
Recording satisfaction	$
Closing fee	$
Total	$

HOLDING COSTS	
Item	*Estimated Cost*
Taxes—6 months @ _____	$
Insurance	$
UTILITIES	
Oil	$
Gas	$
Electric	$
Water	$
Cost of Money $_____ @ _____% interest	$
6 months interest	$
Total	$

ACQUISITION COST	
Item	*Estimated Cost*
Anticipated bid limit	$
COST OF PURCHASE	
Title insurance	$
Recorded deed	$
PROFIT	
Gross profit	$
Minus surprises	$
Net profit	$

Notes: --

APPENDIX C

Standard Buyer's Agreement

Following is what a standard buyer-agency representation agreement looks like. They vary from state to state, but the intent is still the same.

1. Broker's Authorization: Buyer gives Broker the exclusive right to act as Buyer's agent to locate an interest in property and to negotiate the procurement of an interest in property as described in lines _____

(Strike as applicable)

2. Property Type
___ Residential/Personal
___ Residential/Investment
___ Recreational
___ Farm
___ Vacant Land
___ New Construction
___ Other (Identify General Nature of Property)

Check all that Apply

3. Nature of Interest:
___ Purchase
___ Leasehold
___ Option
___ Other

4. Property Characteristics: Purchase Price

Range _____

Other Terms:

_____

_____

_____

(Identify Material Characteristics/Transaction Terms, e.g. Property Size, Location, Occupancy, Interests, Etc.)

Excluded Properties: The following properties are excluded from this Agreement until ___ (Insert Date)

5. Compensation: Broker's compensation shall be: (Check Success Fee, Other Compensation, or Both, as Applicable)

___ SUCCESS FEE _____ percent of the purchase price or

___ OTHER COMPENSATION: (Insert the amount and type of other fee, e.g., Retainer Fee, or Hourly Fee)

If this Agreement calls for a success fee, it is agreed that Broker has earned the success fee if, during the term of this Agreement (or any extension of it), Buyer or any person acting on behalf of Buyer acquires an interest in property or enters into an enforceable written contract between owner and Buyer to acquire an interest in property, and any terms and price acceptable to owner and Buyer. Broker's compensation remains due and payable if an enforceable written contract entered into by Buyer fails to close. Once earned, Broker's compensation is due and payable at the earlier of closing or the date set for closing, unless otherwise agreed to in writing. Broker (may) (may not) (Strike one) accept compensation from owner or owner's agent. Broker's compensation from Buyer will be reduced by any amounts received from owner or owner's agent.

CAUTION: BUYER MAY WORK WITH OWNER OR AGENTS OF THE OWNER IN LOCATING AND NEGOTIATING AN INTEREST IN PROPERTY. HOWEVER, BUYER MAY BE RESPONSIBLE FOR BROKER'S FULL COMPENSATION IF BUYER'S CONTACTS WITH OWNER OR OWNER'S AGENT RESULT IN NO COMPENSATION BEING RECEIVED BY BROKER FROM OWNER OR OWNER'S AGENT.

In consideration for Buyer's agreements, Broker agrees to use professional knowledge and skills, and reasonable efforts, to: 1) locate an interest in property, unless Broker is being retained solely to negotiate the procurement of an interest in a specific property; and 2) negotiate the procurement of an interest in property, as required, by giving advice to Buyer with the scope of Broker's license, facilitating or participating in the discussions of the terms of a potential contract, completing appropriate contractual forms, presenting either party's contractual proposal with an explanation of the proposal's advantages and disadvantages and other efforts including but not limited to the following:

[Unless Broker is retained solely to locate an interest in property:] SHOULD LITIGATION ARISE BETWEEN THE PARTIES IN CONNECTION WITH THIS AGREEMENT, THE PREVAILING PARTY SHALL HAVE THE RIGHT TO REASONABLE ATTORNEY FEES.

Confidentiality Notice: A BROKER IS REQUIRED TO MAINTAIN THE CONFIDENTIALITY OF ALL INFORMATION GIVEN TO THE BROKER IN CONFIDENCE AND OF ALL INFORMATION OBTAINED BY THE BROKER THAT HE OR SHE KNOWS A REASONABLE PARTY WOULD WANT TO BE KEPT CONFIDENTIAL, UNLESS THE INFORMATION IS REQUIRED TO BE DISCLOSED BY LAW. THE FOLLOWING INFORMATION IS REQUIRED TO BE DISCLOSED BY LAW:

1. Material Adverse Facts as Defined by the State Statutes.

2. Any facts known by the Broker that contradict any information included in a written inspection report of the property or real estate that is the subject of the transaction.

IF SIGNED, THIS AGREEMENT CAN CREATE A LEGALLY ENFORCEABLE AGREEMENT. BROKER MAY PROVIDE A GENERAL EXPLANATION OF THE PROVISIONS OF THIS AGREEMENT BUT IS PROHIBITED BY LAW FROM GIVING ADVICE OR OPINIONS CONCERTING YOUR LEGAL RIGHTS UNDER THIS AGREEMENT. AN ATTORNEY SHOULD BE CONSULTED IF LEGAL ADVICE IS NEEDED. BUYER SHOULD CONSULT OTHER EXPERTS AS APPROPRIATE, FOR EXAMPLE, APPRAISERS, TAX ADVISORS, OR HOME INSPECTORS, IF SERVICES BEYOND BROKER'S REAL ESTATE SERVICES ARE NEEDED.

Dated this _____ day of _____, _____

Agent for Broker _____

Broker Firm _____

Broker Address _____

Buyer _____

Buyer Address _____

Buyer Phone _____

Buyer Fax _____

Glossary of Crucial Terms

Adjustable or adjustable interest rate

A mortgage loan that during the last part of its life has an interest rate in effect that is different from the initial or starting interest rate. A very typical adjustable rate mortgage will have an initial or starting interest rate set for two or three years and then will adjust each year thereafter at an interest rate that is determined by adding two numbers together. One of them is the *index* and is a known item, such as the one-year U.S. Treasury Bill interest rate. The other number is the *margin* and is an arbitrary number chosen by the lender as one of the two numbers making up the total interest rate of an adjustable rate mortgage after it adjusts.

The best adjustable rate mortgages, after they adjust in accordance with the above method, are the adjustable rate mortgages that were made for guarantee by Fannie Mae and Freddie Mac. They use consumer-friendly indexes and margins. After adjustment, although the combined rate of index plus margin is somewhat higher than the fixed-interest rates available in the market, the rate is not a terrible one and is affordable to most consumers.

The index plus margin rate on some other adjustable rate mortgages and on all subprime mortgages is terrible. You would want to see only your enemies—your really bad enemies—with such an interest rate. Neither index nor margin is consumer friendly.

The high interest rate after adjustment on all subprime loans and many other adjustable rate mortgage loans is why so many properties, people, neighborhoods, local real estate prices, and local, regional, and the national economy are at risk. It is why so many of the subprime loans made one, two, or three years ago are at such risk of default.

Alt-A loans

Mortgage loans in which one or more borrower or loan characteristics are weaker than required for conforming mortgage loans. These loans typically carry an interest rate roughly .5 percent higher than conforming loans, are a new loan option, and are a huge improvement in loan choice for a borrower facing a choice between high interest rates or no home ownership.

Conforming mortgage loans

Mortgage loans meeting Fannie Mae (FNMA) or Freddie Mac (FHLMC) criteria for guarantee as "standard" or "regular" mortgage loans at attractive rates and terms and conditions.

Deficiency judgment

A court order against a borrower to personally pay the remainder due on a mortgage loan, even though the mortgaged property has been foreclosed. Principal factors for a lender's decision whether or not to seek deficiency judgment include time and cost required, actual prospect for ultimate recovery, and general loan collection policy of the lender.

FHA and VA

Federal Housing Administration and Veterans Administration. These U.S. government agencies are authorized to guarantee low-down-payment (FHA) or no-down-payment (VA) mortgage loans. The VA program was created as a benefit program designed to house the anticipated surge of veterans returning from World War II and as a general stimulus to the economy. The FHA mortgage-loan guarantee program had similar home-ownership and economic-development public-policy objectives.

Fixed rate loans

These are the loans most people think of when they think of a mortgage loan. This type of mortgage loan (most people, even lenders, say "mortgage" when we mean "mortgage loan") is for a set number of years, and the required monthly payment will pay the loan down to zero at the end of the loan term. The most common fixed-rate mortgage loan in the United States is for a thirty-year term.

Flipping

Purchasing a property with the intention of reselling it quickly at a profit, often after making repairs, improvements, and/or upgrades.

FNMA and FHLMC

Federal National Mortgage Association (Fannie Mae) and Federal Home Loan Mortgage Corporation (Freddie Mac). These U.S.-government sponsored entities (GSEs) created under federal law are authorized to guarantee mortgage loans so that local lenders can sell mortgage loans after guarantee and thus continue to have funds for mortgage lending. The GSEs were created with similar home-ownership and economic development objectives as the FHA and VA.

Foreclosure

A legal term for the judicial or quasi-judicial procedure for taking away all rights of ownership of a property from an owner who either purchased a property with a mortgage loan or who owned a property and later borrowed money and signed and gave a mortgage to the lender making the loan.

Interest only

Refers both to a loan type and to a monthly payment. For an initial number of years on an interest-only loan, the required monthly payment is only one-twelfth of the annual interest. (Sometimes this amount is computed monthly.)

Depending on the loan's interest rate, the monthly interest-only payment may be as much as 17 percent or so less than the "full" or "regular" payment. (As the interest rate goes higher, the payment reduction percentage goes lower.)

Equity disappears faster in a declining real estate market with an interest-only loan than with a fixed loan. And the amount that the buyer is upside-down (owing more than the property is worth) grows faster in a declining market as well.

Lien

A lender's or other party's security interest in a property. The most common lien is a mortgage, which is recorded in the public office that handles land recordings. In some states, judgments (court orders to pay) from lawsuits to collect money automatically become liens against property in the county where the lawsuit occurred. In others, a further filing of a judgment in the public office that handles land recordings is necessary for a judgment to become a lien against property in a particular county. Real estate taxes and certain municipal charges for items like trash collection are examples of automatic liens.

Low-doc or no-doc mortgage loans

Low-documentation or no-documentation mortgage loans. These are mortgage loans requiring less documentation of income, assets, or both than traditional lending.

Mortgage

Something signed and given by an owner of a property to a lender giving the lender the right to take the property away if the owner does not repay a loan as agreed or abide by other terms and conditions in the mortgage.

Mortgages usually are recorded in the public office that handles land recordings but may remain unrecorded if a lender so chooses.

Negative amortization or "neg am"

A mortgage loan or mortgage situation in which the outstanding balance is actually getting larger. The lowest monthly payment amount on a payment option loan always results in negative amortization.

Going backward with negative amortization can be a good option if properties are appreciating briskly. It can be ugly if properties are declining in value and very ugly for the borrower, lender, and others if property values are declining sharply.

Although technically *neg am* refers to a mortgage amount that actually grows, if property values are declining or declining sharply, all property owners in a declining market area are going backward as if they had a neg am loan.

People who do not currently own property benefit from declining or declined values. And if 10 percent of us move every year, after a number of years, those who move will have benefited from lower prices if purchasing as well as taking a hit if selling/buying in a lower market.

These effects are not uniform and depend on time, particular market, and the individual situation. But in general, those selling in a declined market and not then buying will really get clobbered.

Since the number of owners and those who sell in a given year far exceed those who buy only in a given year, if markets have declined or decline further, economic losses greatly outweigh gains for those many years. This is one reason we hear so much about possible lower economic growth.

Payment option loans

Relatively new mortgage loan types, first appearing in the first years of the new century. Typically the borrower is given the option of selecting from four monthly payment amounts. The first is a very low monthly payment designed to attract potential borrowers. It always causes negative amortization. The second option is an interest-only payment. The third option is a "regular" or "full" payment. And the fourth option is a higher monthly payment. Please see Chapter 6 for a full discussion of these loans.

Redemption

A legal term meaning the right of a borrower in foreclosure to stop the foreclosure by doing any of the following:

- Bringing the loan completely current, including interest and all costs and fees

- Paying off the entire loan balance, including interest and all costs and fees

Which alternative applies depends on state law and, as a practical matter, on what a local judge will require in a particular foreclosure.

Short sale

The sale of a property in or facing foreclosure to a buyer who does both of the following:

- Pays a cash sum to a borrower who otherwise would be completely wiped out in the foreclosure
- Negotiates with the borrower's lender to accept substantially less than the amount owed to avoid the delays, expenses risks and uncertainties of foreclosure.

Short sale buyers obligate themselves to purchase only if the borrower's lender agrees to accept substantially less than the amount owed and there are no large judgments outstanding that affect title to the property.

Subprime loans and lending

Mortgage loans and lending that does not meet conforming loan standards.

Subprime lending has been with us for a couple of centuries. It grew dramatically from the late 1990s to 2006 or so as investment money poured in.

Subprime lending was integral to the Great Real Estate Boom supporting historically high home-ownership rates, climbing real estate prices, and speculation in real estate. The virtual demise of subprime lending that followed caused a contraction in home-ownership rates, real estate prices, and speculation.

This collapse of subprime lending in 2007 also had huge consequences for financial market instability, personal and investment losses, and legislative and regulatory responses by the White House, Federal Reserve, Congress, and state legislatures.

All of these economic, political, and even social consequences will be with us for many, many years. They will prove to be as powerful as the tidal wave of financially distressed and foreclosed real estate currently affecting us.

It goes without saying that all of this makes full knowledge of lending, real estate, financially distressed real estate, and real estate foreclosures absolutely essential knowledge for all who need to make good personal economic and public policy decisions in the years ahead.

Index

Abandoned houses, 43, 82–83
Adjustable rate mortgages (ARMs), 35, 164–65
Agent relationships, 88–90
Agreements, 45–46, 49–50, 63–65, 88–90, 159–63
Alt-A loans, xiii, 36, 165
Appraisals, 55–56, 102–3
Aptitude, 127–28
Attorneys, 27, 31–32, 58, 61–65, 79–82, 98–99
Auctions
    and bidders, 92–94, 106–9
    foreclosure auctions, 51, 75–76, 79–81
    and other costs, 94–97
    and sales, 79–81
    tax sale auctions, 42–44
Ayer, Don, xiv, 16

Bear markets, 131–34
Bear Stearns, xii
Bidding, 92–94, 106–9. *See also* Auctions
Borrower options, 30–32
Breach of contract, 45–46
Bush, George W., 141
Buyer-agency contracts, 88–90, 159–63

Checklist for properties, 151–58
Climbers, 74, 75
Commercials, 122–28
Conforming loans, 36, 165
Congress, 6, 7, 14, 15, 171
Contracts, 45–46, 88–90, 159–63

Contracts, breach of, 45–46
Cost-of-purchase checklist, 109, 151–58

Dallow, Ted, xiv
Decision-making, 135–38
Deed In Lieu Of Foreclosure Agreement, 16, 31, 47–51
Deficiency judgment, 29, 121, 165
Dot-coms, 10, 11, 132–33, 138

Early mortgage payoff, 38
Emotional attachment, 67–69
Equity sharing, 65–66

"Factors," 78–79
Fannie Mae, xiii, 6–8, 141, 165–67
Fear, 131–35
Federal Home Loan Mortgage Corporation (FHLMC), xiii, 6–8, 141, 165–67
Federal Housing Administration (FHA), 7–8, 40–41, 62, 124, 141, 166
Federal National Mortgage Association (FNMA), xiii, 6–8, 141, 165–67
Federal Reserve, xi–xv, 11–15, 140, 171
Federal Reserve Open Market Committee, xii, 12–14
Fee policy, 80
FHA, 7–8, 40–41, 62, 124, 141, 166
Financial fears, 131–35
Financing, 76–78. *See also* Loans
Financing fads, 137–38

Fixed rate loans, 34, 36, 166
Flipping, 60, 74, 166
Foreclosure Agreement, 49–50
Foreclosure attorney, 31, 58. *See also* Attorneys
Foreclosure auction, 51, 75–76, 79–81
Foreclosures
  alternatives to, 71–73
  buying, 26–32
  deeds in lieu of, 16, 31, 47–51
  definition of, 167
  human cost of, 15–17
  locating, 61–62
  reasons for, 40–46
  sales of, 91–97
  stages of, 57–59
  statistics on, xi–xiii
  Web sites on, 61–62, 139
For sale by owner (FSBO), 86–87
Forty-year fixed-rate loans, 36
Freddie Mac, xiii, 6–8, 141, 165–67
Frequently asked questions, 143–49
Full service brokerage, 87–90

GI Bill, 124
Ginnie Mae, xiii, 6–8
Glossary of terms, 164–71
Government National Mortgage Association (GNMA), xiii, 6–8
Government-sponsored entities (GSEs), 6–9, 166–67
Great Depression, 16, 43
Great Real Estate Boom, xi–xii, 10–11, 134, 170–71
Great Real Estate Bust, 10
Great Real Estate Fall, 10
Great Subprime Lending Boom, 20. *See also* Subprime lending
Greed, 131–35

Hard-money lenders, 78–79
Holdover occupancy, 98–99
Home equity loan, 3, 76–77, 101, 126

Home inspections, 67, 81–84
Homeowners, 3–4

Information gathering, 101–5
Inspections, 81–84
Inspector reports, 81–82
Insurance, 21, 27, 41, 49, 57–59, 80–81, 95–96
Interest-only loan, 34, 40, 77, 167
Interest rates, xi–xii, 11–14, 34–38, 123, 133, 140–42, 164–65
Internet, 61–63, 132, 139
Investment properties
  bid price for, 106–7
  cost concerns of, 108–9
  managing, 117–21
  renting, 117–21
  repairs on, 107
  researching, 110–12
  and tenants, 113–16
  and time requirements, 112–13

Junior liens, 58, 84–85, 94

Knowledge, acquiring, 67–69

Lawyers, 27, 31–32, 58, 61–65, 79–82, 98–99
Legislatures, 15, 171
Liens, 40, 42, 49, 84–85, 167–68
Limited service brokerage, 86–88, 103
Loans, 21–25, 33–36, 40, 77, 138, 165–69
Low-documentation mortgage loans, 33, 168

Mattress money, 21
Mortgagees, 27–29, 46, 59, 93
Mortgage insurance, 21, 41
Mortgage loans, 5–9, 21–25, 33–36, 40, 77, 138, 165–69
Mortgagors, 26–30, 48, 60–66
Multiple Listing Service (MLS), 56, 86–87, 89, 102, 104, 106

NASDAQ, 132–33
Negative amortization, 34, 168–69
Nesters, 74–75
No-documentation mortgage loans, 21–23, 33, 138, 168
Nonmonetary default, 45–46

Pas, Dick, xiv
Payment option loans, 33–36, 169
Personality, 127–28
Preforeclosure
   agreements on, 63–65
   contacting mortgagors for, 60–61
   and equity sharing, 65–66
   finding properties, 62–63
Private mortgage insurance (PMI), 21, 41
Property checklists, 151–58
Property inspections, 67, 81–82
"Pros," 74, 76, 92

Real estate agent relationships, 88–90
Real Estate Boom, xi–xii, xiv, 10–11, 24, 134
Redemption, 28–29, 32, 43, 169–70
Reduced-documentation loans, 23–25, 33
Referee's deed, 96
Refinancing, 38, 39, 77–78
Renting, 117–21
Repairs, 107, 110–12

Sale preparations, 86–90
Sales, following, 98–105
Sales and bidding, 92–94, 106–9. See also Auctions
Sales process, 91–97
Seminars, 122–28
September 11, 2001, xi, 10–11, 132
Septic system, 100
Sheriff's deed, 96
Sheriff's sales, 44–45
Short sales, 30, 70–73, 170
Single-family homes, xii, 3

Statistics, xi–xiii, 3–4, 133–34, 139–42
Stock market, 14, 16, 132–33, 139–40. See also Wall Street
Subprime borrowers, 20–21
Subprime lending, xi–xiv, 7, 9, 20–25, 41, 139–40, 170–71
Subprime mortgages, 11, 22–23, 138–40, 165
Surplus money, 94

Tax sale auctions, 42–44
Tenants, 59, 113–21
Terrorist attacks, xi, 10–11, 132
Title insurance companies, 80–81, 96–97
Title insurance letter reports, 58
Title insurance policies, 27, 49, 57–59, 80–81, 95–97

Uniform Residential Appraisal Report, 55
Upset price, 93–94

Vandalism, 48, 72, 82, 92, 99–100, 111–12
Veterans Administration (VA), 7–8, 61–62, 166

Wall Street, xii, 9, 12, 20, 23–24, 131–34. See also Stock market
Wall Street Journal, xii
Web sites, 61–62, 139
Wells, 100
World War II, 8, 40, 124

Zoning laws, 15, 83–84, 96–97

About the Authors

THEODORE J. DALLOW was the owner of three Century 21 real estate offices in Nassau County, New York. He was the managing broker for HUD foreclosed properties in southern Nassau County.

DON AYER holds a B.A. degree in English from the University of Wisconsin–Platteville. Since 1980, he has sold real estate and foreclosed real estate with local and national firms, as well as his own firm, and he continues to sell real estate with a major national firm. His direct speaking and writing styles delight his colleagues and frustrate those who find refuge in too many words. Don's military service included three years with the Air Defense Command of the U.S. Army.

DICK PAS is an attorney, licensed real estate broker, and co-owner and president of a mid-sized mortgage banking firm, approaching it first billion in loan production. Previously, he served as an attorney with the U.S. Small Business Administration, with duties including foreclosure and bankruptcy matters. In addition, he was an economic analyst with the Congressional Research Service, Library of Congress, and a captain in the U.S. Army Reserves. He holds a B.A. in Economics from Williams College, and his J.D. is from the University of Wisconsin.